The DOCTRINE of the LAST THINGS

The DOCTRINE of the LAST THINGS

Lectures on Christian Hope, Resurrection, and Judgment

SCOTT K. THOMAS II

WAVERLY OAKS
PRESS
Paducah, Kentucky

Copyright © 2026 Scott K. Thomas II

All rights reserved. No part of this book may be reproduced, stored in a retrieval system, or transmitted in any form or by any means—electronic, mechanical, photocopying, recording, or otherwise—without prior written permission of the publisher, except for brief quotations in reviews or scholarly works.

Published by Waverly Oaks Press
An imprint dedicated to biblical, theological, and pastoral instruction.

First edition, 2026.

ISBN: 979-8-9948917-0-4 (paperback)

Scripture quotations are from *The Holy Bible, English Standard Version ® (ESV®)*.
Copyright © 2001 by Crossway, a publishing ministry of Good News Publishers.
Used by permission. All rights reserved.

Printed in the United States of America

Contents

Preface

INTRODUCTION   1

PART ONE: The Shape of Christian Hope
   Chapter 1 Eschatology Defined:
                  The Doctrine of the Last Things 11

PART TWO: The Kingdom Purposes of God
   Chapter 2 The Kingdom of God in
                  Redemptive History 23

   Chapter 3 The "Already" and the "Not Yet"
                  of Christ's Reign 33

   Chapter 4 The Millennium and the Reign of Christ 41

   Chapter 5 The Renewal of Creation:
                  The New Heavens and the New Earth 49

PART THREE: Life Beyond the Grave
   Chapter 6 Death and the Hope of Life Beyond
                  the Grave 59

   Chapter 7 Heaven:
                  Eternal Life in the Presence of God 69

   Chapter 8 Hell: Final Separation from God 77

   Chapter 9 Those Who Have Never Heard:
                  The Question of the Unevangelized 85

PART FOUR: The Return of Christ
 Chapter 10 The Second Coming of Jesus Christ   95

 Chapter 11 The Rapture:
      Interpretations and Implications   103

 Chapter 12 The Tribulation and
      the Climactic Struggle of History   111

PART FIVE: Judgment and the Eternal State
 Chapter 13 The Final Judgment Before God   121

 Chapter 14 The Eternal Blessedness of
      the Righteous   133

 Chapter 15 The Judgment of the Wicked   143

CONCLUSION   153

Endnotes   163

Selected Bibliography and Works Consulted   179

Preface

As a pastor in a Southern Baptist church, I have learned that questions about "the end of the story" are never far from the hearts of God's people. They show up in hospital rooms and funeral homes, in counseling sessions and Sunday school classes. They surface in the quiet questions after a sermon, or in the anxious eyes of a teenager who has just heard about the Second Coming for the first time:

What happens the moment I die?
Will I recognize my loved ones in heaven?
Is hell real—and if so, how could a loving God send anyone there?
How do I make sense of all the talk about the rapture, the tribulation, and the millennium?

These are real questions. They are the questions of parents who have buried a child, of saints who are suffering, of believers trying to remain faithful in a world that often seems to be unraveling.

This book grew out of a series of Wednesday evening lectures delivered to Lone Oak First Baptist Church between August 2025 and January 2026. What began as pastoral teaching for our congregation—helping church members think carefully, biblically, and faithfully about what Scripture teaches concerning the last things—became something that could serve the wider body of Christ. In revising these lectures for publication, I have sought to preserve the clarity and pastoral concern that shaped the original teaching while strengthening the structure and argumentation appropriate for a book.

My prayer is that these pages will help you grow in understanding and also in confidence, patience, and joyful expectation. Eschatology is not given to satisfy curiosity or fuel speculation; it is given to anchor our hope. The New Testament presents the doctrine of last things as a source of endurance and holiness. The return of Christ, the resurrection of the dead, and the renewal of creation are meant to anchor believers in faithful living grounded in the promises of God. When rightly understood, this doctrine shapes how we live today—with courage in suffering, faithfulness in mission, and steady trust that the Lord reigns.

Any work of theology is ultimately an act of service to the church. If these chapters help even one reader trust the faithfulness of God more deeply, endure suffering with greater hope, or live more faithfully in light of Christ's coming kingdom, they will have accomplished their purpose.

May we learn together to echo the final prayer of Scripture: *Amen. Come, Lord Jesus!*

Scott K. Thomas II
Paducah, Kentucky
February 2026

Introduction

Why the Doctrine of Last Things Matters

Christian theology does not end with speculation about the future. It ends with hope—clear, durable confidence in the faithfulness of God. The doctrine of last things (eschatology) addresses the final fulfillment of God's redemptive purposes for creation, humanity, and history itself. Far from being a peripheral doctrine reserved for specialists, eschatology provides the horizon that gives meaning to every other Christian belief.

Scripture presents history as purposeful and directed: God created the world with intention, governs it with wisdom, redeems it through Christ, and will bring all things to a just and glorious conclusion. The doctrine of last things gathers these truths and presses them toward their final outcome. It answers the questions every generation eventually faces: *Where is history going? What happens after death? Will justice prevail? Will God make all things new?*

Defining Christian Eschatology

The word *eschatology* derives from the Greek *eschata* ("last things") and *logos* ("word" or "study"). In Christian theology, eschatology addresses the final fulfillment of God's redemptive purposes—not as speculation about dates and timelines, but as confident hope grounded in what God has already accomplished in Jesus Christ.

Christian eschatology is unique among religious worldviews because the decisive "end" has already entered history through Christ's death, resurrection, and exaltation. The Old Testament looked forward to a future climax in which God would send the Messiah, pour out His Spirit, defeat death, and restore His people. The New Testament declares that these promises *began* to be fulfilled in the life, death, and resurrection of Jesus. Through His resurrection, the future age broke into the present age.

We therefore live *between* Christ's first coming in humility and His second coming in glory, between the "already" of His victory and the "not yet" of its full revelation. The crucifixion and resurrection of Jesus are not merely past events—they are *eschatological* events, God's decisive acts that inaugurate the last days and reconfigure the course of redemptive history. This "already/not yet" framework will guide every chapter that follows.

Why Eschatology Matters for Everyday Discipleship

The Bible never treats the doctrine of last things as mere curiosity. It is always practical. When Paul comforted grieving believers, he explained the coming of Christ and the resurrection of the dead so that they would not "grieve as others do who have no hope" (1 Thess. 4:13). When Peter called the church to holy living, he pointed to the day when the present order will give way to God's renewed creation and urged lives of "holiness and godliness" in light of that coming day (2 Pet. 3:11-13). When John wrote to churches facing pressure and persecution, he did so by unveiling the final victory of the Lamb and the certainty of God's reign.

Eschatology teaches us how to face death, how to endure suffering, how to fight sin, and how to stay faithful in mission. It shows us *where* history is headed—and knowing the end of the story changes how we live in the middle of it.

For conservative evangelical Christians, this is not an abstract concern. Our confession speaks of Christ's return, the resurrection, judgment, heaven, and hell not to satisfy speculation but to shape discipleship. Convictions about the future give urgency to evangelism, sobriety to pastoral care, steadiness in suffering, and hope in the face of death.

Guiding Commitments for These Lectures

Because the doctrine of last things can be easily misused, I have written with several commitments in view.

First, Scripture is our final authority. We will not build our hope on dreams, visions, predictions, or newspaper headlines, but on the written Word of God. Where Scripture speaks plainly, we want to speak plainly. Where Scripture leaves matters less defined, we will resist the temptation to force certainty where God has not given it.

Second, Jesus Christ is at the center. Eschatology is about the King. Jesus came once in humility to save, and He will come again in glory to judge and to reign. Discussions of the rapture, the tribulation, the millennium, heaven, and hell can quickly become detached from Him. In these chapters, the focus repeatedly returns to the person and work of Christ—Savior, King, Judge, and Redeemer.

Third, the aim is pastoral clarity without sensationalism. This work does not attempt to resolve every disputed question, nor does it promote speculative systems built on inference rather than revelation. It seeks to explain what Scripture clearly teaches, to acknowledge where faithful Christians differ, and to encourage humility where God has not spoken exhaustively. Scripture consistently directs believers away from anxious calculation and toward watchful obedience.

Fourth, the approach is conservative evangelical and recognizably Southern Baptist. I write within a tradition that affirms the authority of Scripture, the necessity of personal conversion, salvation by grace through faith in Christ, and the call to holiness and mission. Within those boundaries, I aim to describe major evangelical positions fairly—especially on questions surrounding the rapture, tribulation, and millennium—while teaching what I believe the biblical text most clearly supports.

A Kingdom-Forward Way of Reading the Last Things

One of the great dangers in eschatology is approaching the future in a human-centered way—as if the doctrine exists mainly to satisfy our curiosity, settle our anxieties, help us "decode" world events, or revolve around us. Scripture presents a different center of gravity: *the end is about the kingdom of God in its fullness.* The doctrine of last things is the announcement that God will complete what He began—vindicating His holiness, judging evil, saving His people, renewing creation, and dwelling with them forever.

If the reader approaches eschatology primarily as a set of puzzles to solve, the result will often be speculation or division. But if we approach it as the unveiling of God's kingdom purposes in

Christ, the result is worship, endurance, mission, and hope. The last things are not people-centered; they are God-centered. They are the final public display that the Lord reigns and that His promises do not fail.

This kingdom-focused vision will shape the unfolding doctrine of last things in the chapters that follow. Resurrection serves the renewal of God's creation; judgment vindicates God's holiness and justice; eternal life flows from restored fellowship with the reigning King. Even personal destiny finds its meaning within God's larger purpose: "to reconcile all things to Himself through Christ, making peace by the blood of His cross" (Col. 1:20).

The Purpose and Scope of This Work

This book approaches eschatology as a biblical doctrine to be understood, proclaimed, and lived. While Christians have long debated the timing and sequence of end-time events, Scripture speaks with remarkable clarity about the core realities that shape Christian hope: Jesus Christ will return, the dead will be raised, judgment will occur, evil will be defeated, the righteous will inherit eternal life, and God will dwell with His people forever.

This work does not attempt to resolve every disputed question, nor does it promote speculative systems built on inference rather than revelation. Instead, it seeks to explain what Scripture clearly teaches, to acknowledge where faithful Christians differ, and to encourage humility where God has not spoken exhaustively.

The chapters that follow examine the major themes traditionally associated with the doctrine of last things: the kingdom of God, life after death, the return of Christ, the resurrection, judgment, heaven, hell, and the eternal destinies of the righteous and wicked. Each chapter grounds its claims in the biblical text and situates them within the broader witness of Christian theology. Where interpretive differences arise, the discussion presents the major views fairly while maintaining clear theological boundaries shaped by Scripture.

How the Book is Structured

The organization of this volume reflects a logical and pastoral movement through the major themes of eschatology.

- **Part One: The Shape of Christian Hope** introduces eschatology as a doctrine and sets the framework—kingdom, resurrection, judgment, and new creation.

- **Part Two: The Kingdom Purposes of God** traces the kingdom theme through redemptive history, clarifies the "already" and "not yet" of Christ's reign, considers the millennium, and emphasizes the renewal of creation as the goal of God's saving work.

- **Part Three: Life Beyond Death** addresses the questions most often raised in pastoral ministry—death, the intermediate state, heaven, hell, and the question of those who have never heard the gospel—holding together biblical sobriety and gospel urgency.

- **Part Four: The Return of Christ** focuses on the Second Coming and the major interpretive questions surrounding the rapture and tribulation, with an emphasis on endurance, readiness, and confidence in Christ.

- **Part Five: Judgment and the Eternal State** treats final judgment and the eternal destinies of the righteous and the wicked, seeks to uphold God's justice, and strengthen the church's witness.

A concluding chapter draws the thread together to show that biblical eschatology is a single, Christ-centered hope: God will bring His kingdom in fullness, raise the dead, judge evil, wipe away every tear, and dwell with His people forever.

Eschatology as Christian Formation

The doctrine of last things does more than inform the mind—it shapes the life of faith. Scripture repeatedly connects future hope with present faithfulness. The promise of resurrection strengthens perseverance. The certainty of judgment calls believers to holiness and justice. The hope of eternal life fuels endurance in suffering. The expectation of Christ's return anchors the church in mission.

How I Hope You Will Use This Book

My encouragement is simple: read slowly, think carefully, and keep your heart open before the Lord. As you go, keep asking two questions:

1. *What does this doctrine reveal about the character of God?*

2. *How should this doctrine change the way I live today?*

If, by God's grace, these pages help you love Christ more, long for His coming more, fear sin more, endure suffering more faithfully, and rest more deeply in the promises of God, then they will have fulfilled their purpose.

Eschatology is ultimately about the faithfulness of God. He will complete the good work He began (Phil. 1:6). And as we study the last things together, may we learn to echo the final prayer of Scripture:

Amen. Come, Lord Jesus! (Rev. 22:20).

Part One

The Shape of Christian Hope

Chapter 1

Eschatology and the Kingdom of God

Introduction

The doctrine of last things, commonly called *eschatology*, must be approached first and foremost as a doctrine of God's kingdom. Scripture does not present the end of history as a human-centered resolution to personal questions about death, destiny, or reward; it presents the end as the public, visible, and decisive reestablishment of God's rightful rule over all creation.[1] Eschatology, therefore, is not primarily about what happens to individuals, but about what God accomplishes as King.

When eschatology is approached from a human-centered perspective, it easily becomes distorted. Attention shifts toward speculation, timelines, personal escape, or anxiety about outcomes. Scripture consistently directs attention elsewhere; framing the end of all things as the triumph of God's reign, the vindication of His holiness, and the fulfillment of His covenant purposes.[2] Only within that kingdom-centered framework do questions about resurrection, judgment, and eternal destiny find their proper place.

The term eschatology derives from the Greek words *eschata* ("last things") and *logos* ("word," "study"), and in Christian theology it denotes the study of God's ultimate purposes for creation and redemption. Eschatology answers a foundational theological question: *How will God bring His kingdom to its appointed fullness?*[3] Until that question governs the study of last things, the doctrine loses its power and coherence. Scripture reveals that God is not merely concluding history, but completing it—bringing creation, redemption, and judgment into perfect harmony under His sovereign rule.

Defining the Doctrine of the Last Things

The doctrine of last things describes the final outworking of God's purposes in creation and redemption, including the destiny of humanity and the angelic realm, the renewal of the world, and the establishment of God's eternal kingdom.[4] Eschatology concerns both the end of the present age and the beginning of the age to come. Because God is Creator as well as Redeemer, the last things are not an arbitrary stopping point, but the consummation of the good creation that began in Genesis 1.

Scripture consistently frames history as moving toward a divinely appointed goal. God is not reacting to events within time; He is sovereignly directing history toward its intended conclusion.[5] The Bible presents God as "the Alpha and the Omega, the first and the last, the beginning and the end" (Rev. 22:13), and because God stands at both the beginning and the end of history, the last things give coherence and meaning to everything that precedes them.

Key biblical passages that orient Christian eschatology include Titus 2:11-14, which ties present godliness to future hope; 1 Corinthians 15:50-55, which proclaims the resurrection victory over death; and 1 Thessalonians 4:13-18, which comforts believers with the promise of Christ's return.[6] These texts, together with many others, show that the New Testament treats the future not as a curiosity but as the horizon that shapes Christian faith, holiness, and perseverance.

The End Revealed in the Middle of History

Christian eschatology is unique among religious worldviews because the decisive events of the end have already entered history through the person and work of Jesus Christ.[7] The Old Testament looked forward to a future climax in which God would send the Messiah, pour out His Spirit, defeat death, and restore His people (Isa. 25:6-9; Joel 2:28-32; Daniel 12:1-3).[8] These promises created a hope for personal survival after death, and for a comprehensive renewal of God's people and creation.

The New Testament declares that these promises began to be fulfilled in the life, death, resurrection, and exaltation of Jesus. Christ came "in the fullness of time" (Gal. 4:4), not at the end of history but in its midst. Through His resurrection, the future age broke into the present age. Paul describes Christ as "the firstfruits of those who have fallen asleep" (1 Cor. 15:20), meaning that His resurrection is both a real historical event and a promise of what is still to come.[9] The resurrection is thus the initial installment of the new creation, in which death is decisively defeated and the power of the age to come is made manifest.

Because the end has been revealed in the middle of history, Christian eschatology reflects on realities that have already begun and are still unfolding. The crucifixion and resurrection of Jesus are more than past events; they are eschatological events—God's decisive acts that inaugurate the last days and reconfigure the course of redemptive history.[10] Hebrews affirms that God "has spoken to us by his Son" in "these last days" (Heb. 1:2) and that

Christ "has appeared once for all at the end of the ages" to put away sin by His sacrifice (Heb. 9:26). The church, therefore, lives in light of a future that has already begun to dawn in Christ.

This Christ-centered perspective safeguards eschatology from being reduced to speculation about unknown dates or obscure symbols. Instead, the focus falls on what God has definitively done in Jesus and on how that work anticipates and guarantees the final consummation. As many modern biblical theologians have observed, Christology and eschatology thus belong together: to speak of who Christ is and what he has done is already to speak of how God is bringing history to its appointed goal.

As a result, Christian eschatology is not concerned only with distant future events. It reflects on realities that have already begun and are still unfolding. The end has, in a real sense, already happened in the middle of history, and the church now lives between fulfillment and consummation.

Personal and Cosmic Eschatology

Eschatology addresses two closely related dimensions of God's purposes: *personal eschatology* and *cosmic eschatology*. Personal eschatology concerns the destiny of individual human beings—death, the intermediate state, resurrection, and final judgment.[11] Scripture teaches that death does not end human existence, but introduces a temporary state while history continues toward its conclusion (Luke 23:43; Phil. 1:23). Believers who die are "away from the body and at home with the Lord" (2 Cor. 5:8), awaiting the resurrection of the body and the public vindication of God's people.

Cosmic eschatology, by contrast, concerns the destiny of creation as a whole. It includes themes such as the kingdom of God, the defeat of evil, the resurrection of all the dead, and the renewal of heaven and earth (Rom. 8:18-25; Rev. 21:1-5).[12] The biblical story anticipates the transformation of the world, as God brings forth "new heavens and a new earth" where righteousness dwells (2 Pet. 3:13).

These two dimensions are inseparable. Individual destiny cannot be fully understood apart from God's purposes for the world, and God's renewal of creation includes the redemption and glorification of His people. The period between personal death and the final consummation—often called the *intermediate state*—highlights the tension of living between what has already been accomplished in Christ and what remains to be completed at His return.[13] A kingdom-centered eschatology thus corrects both individualistic reductions of Christian hope and impersonal visions of cosmic renewal by holding together the person and the cosmos in the purpose of the triune God.

Old Testament Foundations of the Kingdom of God

The New Testament proclamation of the kingdom of God rests firmly on foundations laid in the Old Testament. From the beginning of Scripture, God reveals Himself as King over creation (Gen. 1:1; Ps. 24:1), yet the biblical story quickly shows that His kingship is challenged by human rebellion.[14] Eschatological hope in the Old Testament arises from God's promise to reassert His righteous rule in a decisive and visible way, restoring His creation and His people.

A central strand of this hope is found in the *Davidic covenant*. God's promise to David that his throne would be established forever (2 Sam. 7:12-16; Ps. 89:3-4) shaped Israel's expectation of a coming king whose reign would bring justice, peace, and faithfulness. Later prophets built upon this promise, speaking of a future ruler from David's line who would reign in righteousness over a restored people (Isa. 9:6-7; Jer. 23:5-6).[15] The messianic king would embody God's rule, shepherd His people, and judge the nations.

The book of Daniel provides one of the clearest Old Testament visions of the coming kingdom. Daniel 2 portrays a succession of human kingdoms that will ultimately be replaced by a kingdom established by God Himself—a kingdom that "shall never be destroyed" (Dan. 2:44). In Daniel 7, this kingdom is associated with "one like a son of man," who receives everlasting dominion from the Ancient of Days (Dan. 7:13-14).[16] These visions establish both the divine origin and the eternal character of God's kingdom, while also linking it to a messianic figure who represents the faithful people of God.

The prophets also spoke of the kingdom in terms of restoration, universality, and renewal. Isaiah envisioned a future in which God would reign on Mount Zion, bringing peace among the nations and the renewal of creation itself (Isa. 2:1-4; 11:1-9).[17] The nations would stream to the Lord's mountain to receive His instruction, and the wolf would dwell with the lamb in a renewed creation shaped by the knowledge of the Lord. The psalms celebrate the coming reign of the Lord as a time when righteousness will flourish, justice will be done for the oppressed, and the nations will rejoice (Ps. 96; Ps. 98).

Together, these texts show that the Old Testament does more than anticipate isolated end-time events; it anticipates the arrival of God's kingly rule in fullness—a reign that defeats evil, restores God's people, and renews the world. The kingdom is thus both God's active rule and the realm in which that rule is gladly acknowledged. These expectations form the theological backdrop for Jesus' announcement of the kingdom in the New Testament and provide the deep roots for a kingdom-centered doctrine of last things.

The Kingdom of God as the Framework of Eschatology

At the center of biblical eschatology stands the theme of the kingdom of God. Jesus announced that "the time is fulfilled, and the kingdom of God is at hand" (Mark 1:15), thereby declaring that God's long-promised reign has begun to manifest itself in history. The kingdom of God refers to God's sovereign rule exercised over His creation, especially as that rule is revealed and enacted in His redemptive purposes. While God has always been King in an absolute sense (Ps. 103:19), the Bible describes a redemptive form of His reign that unfolds progressively through covenant, promise, and fulfillment.[18]

The coming of Christ inaugurated this kingdom but did not bring it to its final form.[19] In His earthly ministry, Jesus proclaimed the kingdom in word and deed, forgiving sins, casting out demons, healing the sick, and raising the dead as signs that God's royal power was breaking into a world enslaved to sin, death, and the devil. George Eldon Ladd summarizes this biblical picture by describing the kingdom as God's dynamic rule rather than a merely spatial realm, a reign that has entered history in anticipation of its final consummation.

The kingdom of God is also profoundly Trinitarian in character. The Father sends the Son to announce and inaugurate the kingdom; the Son accomplishes redemption through the cross and resurrection; and the Holy Spirit applies the benefits of Christ's work, gathers and empowers the church, and serves as the pledge of the inheritance that will be fully revealed at the end. The Spirit's presence in the people of God is described as "firstfruits" and "guarantee" of what is to come (Rom. 8:23; Eph. 1:13-14), underscoring that the life of the kingdom is already operative in the community of believers.

Within this framework, the church is not the kingdom itself, but it is the community that lives under God's reign and bears witness to the coming fullness of His rule. The church proclaims the gospel of the kingdom, embodies its values in holiness and justice, and anticipates its final revelation through worship, mission, and sacrificial love. By locating eschatology within the kingdom of God, Scripture calls believers to view the future not as an escape from the world, but as the consummation of God's redemptive work in and for the world. This kingdom-focused vision will shape the unfolding doctrine of last things in the chapters that follow.

Conclusion

The doctrine of last things calls the church to see history through the lens of God's kingdom. Scripture teaches that the end of the age does not center on human fear, curiosity, or speculation, but on the public triumph of Gods righteous rule. Eschatology proclaims that the kingdom promised throughout the Old Testament, inaugurated in Jesus Christ, and proclaimed by the church will one day be fully and visibly established.[20]

This kingdom-centered vision reshapes how believers understand every aspect of the last things. Resurrection serves the renewal of God's creation; judgment vindicates God's holiness and justice; eternal life flows from restored fellowship with the reigning King. Even personal destiny finds its meaning within God's larger purpose to reconcile all things to Himself through Christ: "making peace by the blood of his cross" (Col. 1:20). [21]

Because the end has already broken into history through Jesus, believers live with confidence rather than fear and faithfulness rather than speculation. The study of eschatology therefore directs the church away from human-centered anxiety and toward God-centered hope. The kingdom of God stands as the true center of Christian expectation—the assurance that the faithful God who began His work in creation and redemption will bring it to completion in glory.

Part Two

The Kingdom Purposes of God

Chapter 2

The Kingdom of God in Redemptive History

Introduction

Few themes are as central to the teaching of Jesus as the kingdom of God. The Gospels repeatedly describe Jesus proclaiming, explaining, and embodying God's kingdom, and He presents it as the fulfillment of Israel's long-standing hopes. To understand Christian eschatology rightly, the kingdom of God must be understood as a redemptive reality unfolding through history and reaching its decisive turning point in the person and work of Jesus Christ.

This chapter explores the kingdom of God as it emerges from the Old Testament, is announced, and enacted by Jesus, and moves toward its final consummation. In doing so, it clarifies the relationship between the kingdom, the church, and the future hope of God's people, showing that the kingdom is the central thread that unites the whole story of redemption.

Defining the Kingdom of God

The kingdom of God refers to the rule and reign of God over His creation as its rightful King. While God has always been sovereign over all things (Ps. 103:19), Scripture speaks of a redemptive manifestation of His rule that is established, opposed, advanced, and finally consummated within history.[22] The kingdom is therefore more than a place or a people; it is God's active reign exercised according to His saving purposes.

In biblical language, then, "kingdom" refers first to God's reign—His royal authority—and only secondarily to the realm or sphere in which that reign is acknowledged.[23] God's kingly rule creates and transforms a realm: a redeemed people and, ultimately, a renewed creation in which His will is done on earth as it is in heaven. This understanding guards against reducing the kingdom to a geographical territory, to a purely inward spiritual experience, or to any single human institution, including the church.[24]

God's kingly reign has both structure and purpose. It is structured through covenant, promise, and fulfillment, as God progressively reveals and enacts His kingship in the history of Israel and in the coming of Christ. It is directed toward the ultimate goal of restoring creation under God's righteous rule, so that "the earth will be filled with the knowledge of the glory of the Lord as the waters cover the sea" (Hab. 2:14). In this sense, the kingdom provides the framework within which all eschatological doctrines find their coherence.

Old Testament Roots of Kingdom Expectation

The Old Testament lays essential groundwork for the New Testament proclamation of the kingdom. God reveals Himself early as King over creation—"in the beginning, God created the heavens and the earth" (Gen. 1:1)—and the psalmist affirms, "The earth is the Lord's and the fullness thereof, the world and those who dwell therein" (Ps. 24:1). Yet human rebellion introduces disorder and alienation, and the promise of a future restored reign of God emerges as a central hope.

An early glimpse of this hope appears in Genesis 14, where Abram encounters Melchizedek, "king of Salem," and "priest of God Most High" (Gen. 14:18-20). Hebrews reflects on this figure:

> For this Melchizedek, king of Salem, priest of the Most High God, met Abraham returning from the slaughter of the kings and blessed him, and to him Abraham apportioned a tenth part of everything. He is first, by translation of his name, king of righteousness, and then he is also king of Salem, that is, king of peace." (Heb. 7:1-2)

This mysterious king-priest, later associated with an enduring priesthood and royal authority, points forward to a ruler whose reign is grounded in righteousness, peace, and divine appointment.[25] The New Testament sees this pattern fulfilled in Jesus, the one who is "a priest forever, after the order of Melchizedek" (Heb. 5:6), uniting kingship and priesthood in His person and grounding the permanence of the eschatological kingdom in His eternal office.[26]

The Eden narrative also anticipates the kingdom by portraying humanity as vice-regents under God's rule, called to exercise dominion over creation (Gen. 1:26-28). Israel's later life as a covenant people, especially under the Davidic monarchy, becomes a historical embodiment—though imperfect and temporary—of God's kingship in the world.[27] The Davidic covenant further sharpens Israel's kingdom expectation. God's promise to establish David's throne forever (2 Samuel 7:12-16) creates anticipation of a future king whose reign would embody justice, peace, and faithfulness. Prophets such as Isaiah and

Jeremiah describe this coming ruler in unmistakably messianic terms:

> Of the increase of his government and of peace there will be no end, on the throne of David and over his kingdom, to establish it and to uphold it with justice and with righteousness from this time forth and forever. (Isa. 9:7)

> Behold, the days are coming, declares the Lord, when I will raise up for David a righteous Branch, and he shall reign as king and deal wisely, and shall execute justice and righteousness in the land. (Jer. 23:5)

The Psalms contribute to this vision through royal and messianic psalms that portray the king's reign in expansive, even cosmic, terms. Psalm 2, for example, speaks of the Lord's anointed ruling the nations: "Ask of me, and I will make the nations your heritage, and the ends of the earth your possession" (Ps. 2:8), a text later applied directly to Christ in the New Testament (Acts 4:25-28; Heb. 1:5).

Taken together, the Old Testament presents a redemptive—historical arc of the kingdom. In Eden, God's kingship is expressed through human stewardship; in Israel, His rule takes the form of a covenant nation and a Davidic throne; in the prophets and psalms, hope shifts toward a future, universal reign through a messianic king; and in the wisdom and apocalyptic literature, God's final victory over evil and His everlasting dominion are anticipated in vivid imagery (e.g., Dan. 2; 7). These expectations set the stage for the appearance of Jesus as "the son of David" and the bearer of the kingdom.[28]

The Kingdom Proclaimed and Revealed by Jesus

Against this Old Testament backdrop, Jesus appears announcing that the long-awaited kingdom has drawn near.[29] His preaching begins with the declaration, "The time is fulfilled, and the kingdom of God is at hand; repent and believe in the gospel" (Mark 1:15). This announcement signals that God's redemptive rule is now breaking into history in a new and decisive way.

Jesus explains the nature of the kingdom primarily through parables. In Matthew 13, he describes the kingdom as both hidden and powerful, growing quietly yet irresistibly, like seed in a field or yeast in dough (Matt. 13:24-52). These images emphasize that the kingdom does not arrive with immediate outward splendor but advances according to God's timing and purpose, often in ways that remain concealed from human expectation.[30] The kingdom is present in Jesus' words and deeds, yet its full manifestation awaits a future unveiling.

Jesus also teaches that entrance into the kingdom requires humility, repentance, and childlike faith (Matt. 18:1-4). Possession of religious status or moral achievement does not secure participation; rather, the kingdom is received as a gift from the King Himself.

The Gospels further portray the kingdom as manifested in Jesus' miracles, exorcisms, and acts of mercy.[31] When John the Baptist questions whether Jesus is the coming One, Jesus points to the signs of the kingdom:

> Go and tell John what you hear and see: the blind receive their sight and the lame walk, lepers are cleansed and the deaf hear, and the dead are raised up, and the poor have good news preached to them. (Matt. 11:4-5)

These signs anticipate the age to come and reveal that God's royal power is already at work in Jesus' ministry, pushing back the effects of sin and brokenness. The kingdom, therefore, is not an abstract concept but a concrete reality embodied in the King's words, works, and presence.

The Kingdom, the Church, and the World

Because Jesus reigns by His Spirit, the kingdom of God is present wherever Christ's authority is acknowledged.[32] For this reason, the church has an intimate relationship to the kingdom, yet the two are not identical. The church is the community of those who have submitted to Christ's reign and bear witness to the kingdom in the present age. Jesus grants to His disciples "the keys of the kingdom of heaven" (Matt. 16:19), indicating that the church is entrusted with proclaiming the message that opens and closes the door to participation in the kingdom.

The kingdom, however, extends beyond the visible boundaries of the church. While the church proclaims and embodies kingdom values, the kingdom itself represents the final result of God's redemptive work when all things are brought into submission to Christ (1 Cor. 15:24-28). George Eldon Ladd, for example, emphasizes that the kingdom is fundamentally God's reign and that the church is the fellowship of those who have already entered that reign. In this sense, the church is a sign, instrument, and foretaste of the kingdom:

- *Sign*: The church points beyond itself to the coming reign of God, displaying in its life together a preview of the future order of righteousness, peace, and joy.

- *Instrument*: The church is used by God in the present age to advance His redemptive purposes through proclamation, service, and witness.

- *Foretaste*: The church anticipates the life of the age to come, experiencing even now the blessings of God's rule through the presence of the Spirit, the fellowship of believers, and the hope of glory.[33]

Other theologians, such as Geerhardus Vos, have argued for a closer identification between the kingdom and the church, especially in terms of the invisible church composed of all true believers.[34] While recognizing this important perspective, the approach taken here follows the distinction that the kingdom is Christ's royal rule and the church is the community formed by that rule and commissioned to testify to it. This guards against equating the kingdom with any particular visible structure, denomination, or cultural program, and keeps the focus on the living reign of the King.

This kingdom perspective also carries profound missional and ethical implications.[35] The kingdom is characterized by righteousness, justice, mercy, and reconciliation, and the church is called to embody these realities in its communal life and public witness. Kingdom theology therefore resists both a purely inward, spiritualized understanding of Christian faith and a merely political reduction of the gospel to social program. Instead, it summons believers to live under Christ's lordship in every sphere of life, bearing witness to the coming reign through holiness, love, and service in the world.

Jesus' instruction to pray, "Your kingdom come, your will be done, on earth as it is in heaven" (Matt. 6:10), underscores both the present and future dimensions of this reality. Believers live under Christ's reign now, yet they continue to long for the day when God's rule will be universally acknowledged and fully realized.

The King Revealed Through Humility and the Cross

One of the most striking features of Jesus' teaching is the way His kingship is revealed through humility rather than political power. He enters Jerusalem riding on a donkey (Matt. 21:1-9), fulfilling prophetic expectation while subverting popular assumptions about royal authority. His kingdom advances through suffering obedience, not through coercion or worldly domination.[36]

This paradox reaches its climax at the cross. The inscription placed above Jesus – "King of the Jews" (Luke 23:38) — was intended as mockery, yet it proclaimed a profound theological truth. Jesus reigns by giving His life, conquering sin and death through self-sacrificial love. The Gospel narratives present the crucifixion as a strange enthronement, with the King lifted up, crowned with thorns, and publicly displayed, revealing the true character of God's royal authority.

The New Testament insists that the kingdom's future glory is inseparable from the cruciform character of the King. The book of Revelation portrays the exalted Christ reigning in glory as the Lamb who was slain:[37]

> Then I saw heaven opened, and behold, a white horse! The one sitting on it is called Faithful and True, and in righteousness he judges and makes war... On his robe and on his thigh he has a name written, King of kings and Lord of lords. (Rev. 19:11, 16)

The same Jesus who reigns in humility from the cross will be revealed in majesty as the King of kings and Lord of lords. His kingdom, therefore, is both cruciform and victorious, marked by sacrificial love and final, public triumph over evil.

Conclusion

The kingdom of God is the central thread that unites biblical eschatology. Rooted in Old Testament promise, revealed in Jesus Christ, and moving toward final consummation, the kingdom provides the framework for understanding God's purposes in history. From Eden's original commission, through Israel's story and the hope of a Davidic Messiah, to the preaching, miracles, death, and resurrection of Jesus, God has been unveiling His plan to restore His reign over all things.[38]

Christians live in the midst of this redemptive history as the church called to live under Christ's reign and to bear witness to His kingdom in the world. The church is not itself the kingdom, but it is the community created by the King's rule, serving as sign, instrument, and foretaste of the coming order in which God will be "all in all" (1 Cor. 15:28).[39]

Believers therefore stand between inauguration and fulfillment—called to faithful obedience under Christ's present reign while longing and praying for the day when the kingdom will come in fullness and every knee will bow and every tongue confess that Jesus Christ is Lord (Phil. 2:10-11). This tension prepares the way for the next chapter's exploration of the "already" and the "not yet" of Christ's reign.

Chapter 3

The "Already" and the "Not Yet" of Christ's Reign

Introduction

One of the most important insights for understanding the kingdom of God is the recognition that it is both a present reality and a future hope. The New Testament consistently speaks of the kingdom as something that has already arrived through Jesus Christ, while at the same time directing believers to pray, hope, and wait for its full manifestation.[40] This tension—commonly described as the "already" and the "not yet"—is not a problem to be solved, but a biblical pattern to be understood.

This chapter explores how the kingdom of God can be genuinely present in Christ's ministry while still awaiting final consummation. By tracing Jesus' teaching and the church's experience, we will see how this framework provides clarity, balance, and hope for Christian faith and life.[41]

Defining the "Already" and the "Not Yet"

The "already/not yet" framework affirms that the kingdom of God has been inaugurated in the person and work of Jesus Christ but will not be consummated until His return in glory.[42] The decisive act of God's reign has begun, yet its final effects are still unfolding within history.

When Jesus announced, "The time is fulfilled, and the kingdom of God is at hand; repent and believe in the gospel" (Mark 1:14-15), he declared that God's saving rule had entered the present age. At the same time, Jesus taught His disciples to pray, "Your kingdom come" (Matt. 6:10), clearly indicating that the kingdom had not yet arrived in its fullness. Both statements are true, and together they shape the Christian understanding of eschatology.

Other New Testament passages reinforce this dual perspective. Believers are said to have been "delivered from the domain of darkness and transferred to the kingdom of his beloved Son" (Col. 1:13), and to be seated with Christ in the heavenly places (Eph. 2:6), even as they still "groan inwardly as we wait eagerly for adoption as sons, the redemption of our bodies" (Rom. 8:23). The kingdom is present in hidden, anticipatory form, while its public, visible reality awaits the day when Christ returns and "every knee should bow... and every tongue confess that Jesus Christ is Lord" (Phil. 2:10-11).[43]

Evangelical theologians from differing millennial perspectives—historic premillennial, amillennial, and some modified dispensational—have used this "already/not yet" language to describe the New Testament pattern, even as they diverge on how certain prophetic details are to be understood.[44] In what follows, the focus will remain on those aspects of the framework that rest on clear biblical teaching.

Historical Approaches to the Kingdom

Throughout church history, Christians have wrestled with how to hold together the present and future dimensions of the kingdom. In the modern period, three influential approaches have emerged, each attempting to account for Jesus' teaching and the experience of the early church. These are often described as consistent eschatology, realized eschatology, and inaugurated eschatology.[45] What follows is a descriptive overview rather than an endorsement of any one scholar's system.

Consistent (Thoroughgoing) Eschatology

Consistent eschatology emphasizes the future character of the kingdom. This view is associated with Johannes Weiss and Albert Schweitzer, who argued that Jesus proclaimed the kingdom primarily as an imminent, future event.[46] According to this view, Jesus expected God's reign to arrive decisively within His own generation, and much of His preaching is read as an intense call to prepare for that impending crisis.

Advocates of this approach highlight Jesus' prayers and parables that look toward a coming climax. The petition "Your kingdom come" (Matt. 6:10), along with parables such as the wheat and the weeds (Matt. 13:24-30), the dragnet (Matt. 13:47-50), and the ten virgins (Matt. 25:1-13), all anticipate a future moment when God's rule will be openly revealed. Jesus' description of the Son of Man coming in glory to judge the nations (Matt. 25:31-33) further reinforces this forward-looking emphasis.

From an evangelical perspective, this approach helpfully underscores the reality of future judgment and the necessity of hope beyond this present age. Yet on its own, it does not adequately explain Jesus' claims that the kingdom was already present in His words and works.[47] When taken to an extreme, it can leave the impression that Jesus' expectations failed or that His message was almost entirely focused on a future that did not arrive in the way anticipated, conclusions that conservative interpreters rightly reject.

Realized Eschatology

Realized eschatology, most clearly associated with C.H. Dodd, stresses the present reality of the kingdom. According to this view, the kingdom was fully realized in Jesus' ministry, death, and resurrection; the decisive moment of God's reign had already arrived. The emphasis falls on what God has accomplished now rather than on what still lies ahead.[48]

Jesus' exorcisms provide a key example. When He declares, "If it is by the Spirit of God that I cast out demons, then the kingdom of God has come upon you" (Matt. 12:28), He presents His actions as evidence that Satan's power is already being overthrown. Several parables reinforce this present focus, including the hidden treasure and the pearl of great value (Matt. 13:44-46), which portray the kingdom as something to be discovered and embraced in the present.

The Gospel of John also emphasizes present participation in eternal life. Jesus says, "Whoever hears my word and believes him who sent me has eternal life… he has passed from death to life" (John 5:24). From this perspective, eternal life and kingdom blessing are not simple future promises but present realities for those who believe.

Conservative evangelicals can affirm much of this emphasis on the present work of Christ and the believer's current participation in God's life. However, when realized eschatology minimizes or reinterprets future bodily resurrection, final judgment, or Christ's visible return, it goes beyond the balance of New Testament teaching and departs from the historic Christian hope.[49]

Inaugurated Eschatology

Inaugurated eschatology seeks to hold together both the present and future dimensions of the kingdom. This approach has been especially influential among evangelical scholars such as George Eldon Ladd and Anthony Hoekema, though they differ on some millennial details.[50] According to this view, Jesus inaugurated God's reign during His earthly ministry, but its final completion awaits His return. The kingdom is already present in hidden, partial, and anticipatory form, yet it remains not yet in its fullness, glory, and universal recognition.

A widely used illustration compares Christ's work to the events of World War II. The decisive victory in Europe was secured on D-Day, yet the war did not officially end until V-E Day. In a similar way, Christ achieved decisive victory over sin, death, and Satan through His cross and resurrection, but the full effects of that victory will only be revealed at His second coming.[51] The decisive battle has been won, yet the final surrender of every enemy still lies ahead.

Jesus' teaching fits naturally within this framework. His proclamation in Mark 1:14-15 announces that the kingdom has drawn near, while His parables of growth—the Sower (Luke 8:4-8), the seed growing (Mark 4:26-29), and the mustard seed (Mark 4:30-32)—depict a kingdom that begins quietly, grows over time, and reaches fulfillment at harvest. The kingdom is present in seed form but awaits its full harvest at the end of the age.

Moreover, when the disciples returned rejoicing that demons were subject to them, Jesus declared, "I saw Satan fall like lightning from heaven" (Luke 10:18), revealing that the kingdom was already advancing and that the powers of darkness were being displaced. Yet Jesus also taught that the gospel must be proclaimed to all nations "and then the end will come" (Matt. 24:14). The mission of the church unfolds within this "already/not yet" tension, as the victory of Christ is proclaimed throughout the world while the church waits for His appearing.

Among conservative evangelicals, inaugurated eschatology is often seen as best reflecting the whole of the New Testament witness: affirming a truly present kingdom without weakening the sure expectation of Christ's visible return, bodily resurrection, and final judgment.[52] Within this broad framework, believers may still disagree on specific questions such as the timing and nature of the millennium, the order of end-time events, or the future of Israel. This chapter aims to describe the shared biblical structure rather than to settle those debates.

Living Between Inauguration and Consummation

Inaugurated eschatology helps explain the tension believers feel in daily life. On the one hand, they already experience forgiveness, new birth, and the presence of the Holy Spirit (John 3:3-8; Rom. 8:9-11). They are new creations in Christ (2 Cor. 5:17), and the powers of the age to come have already broken into their lives. On the other hand, they continue to face suffering, opposition, and death. The kingdom is present, but it is not yet complete; Christians live in the overlap of the ages, where the old order is passing away and the new creation has begun.[53]

This tension shapes Christian discipleship in several ways. First, it grounds hope: the future is secure because Christ's victory has already been won. Second, it guards against triumphalism: the church does not expect to escape weakness, suffering, or persecution before Christ's return. Third, it promotes perseverance and holiness: believers are called to live now in light of the coming kingdom, embodying its values of righteousness, justice, and love even in a world that does not yet recognize Christ's lordship.

Evangelical writers have emphasized that this "already/not yet" pattern keeps Christian hope from collapsing into either despair or presumption.[54] When the present brokenness of the world is taken seriously without denying the reality of Christ's victory, the church is freed to serve with realism and courage, confident that "your labor is not in vain in the Lord" (1 Cor. 15:58).

The church therefore lives as a community of hope, bearing witness to the reign of Christ while longing for its visible fulfillment. It proclaims the good news that the kingdom has come near in Jesus, invites people to enter that kingdom through repentance and faith, and waits for the day when the King will appear and make all things new.

Conclusion

The "already" and the "not yet" of the kingdom of God provide a biblically grounded framework for understanding Jesus' teaching and the Christian life.[55] It has truly arrived in Christ, and its power is at work in the world through the Holy Spirit and the witness of the church. At the same time, believers continue to pray, "Your kingdom come," awaiting the day when Christ's reign will be fully revealed, and every enemy will be placed under His feet.

Holding this tension guards the church from both resignation and premature triumphalism. It anchors Christian hope in the finished work of Christ and in the sure promise of His return, calling believers to live faithfully between inauguration and consummation until the King appears in glory.

Chapter 4

The Millennium and the Reign of Christ

Introduction

Few topics within Christian eschatology have generated as much discussion and disagreement as the millennium. For many readers, questions about a future thousand-year reign of Christ immediately raise concerns about symbolism, chronology, and competing interpretive systems. Yet the doctrine of the millennium is not meant to provoke speculation or division. At its core, it addresses a far more fundamental issue: how and when the reign of Christ is fully displayed in history before the final consummation of all things.

This chapter examines the biblical foundations of the millennium, the major interpretive approaches that have developed within the church, and the theological convictions that unite Christians despite their differences. The goal in this chapter is not to settle every disputed detail, but to clarify what Scripture teaches and to situate the millennium within the larger hope of Christ's victorious reign.

Defining the Millennium

The term *millennium* comes from the Latin words *mille* (thousand) and *annus* (year), meaning "a thousand years." In Christian theology, the millennium refers to the period described in Revelation 20:1-10 during which Christ reigns and Satan's power is restrained prior to the final judgment and the renewal of all things.

Closely related to this term is *chiliasm*, derived from the Greek word *chilia* ("thousand"), which likewise refers to belief in a thousand-year reign of Christ. While the terminology is technical, the underlying theological question is straightforward: How should the church understand Christ's reign in relation to the present age and the final state?

It is important to note that Revelation 20 is the only passage in Scripture that explicitly mentions a thousand-year period. For this reason, any faithful interpretation of the millennium must read this passage carefully and in harmony with the rest of biblical teaching on Christ's kingship, resurrection, and final victory. Evangelical systematic theologians such as Millard Erickson emphasize this point: interpretations should be tethered to the clear teaching of Scripture and held with humility where details are less explicit.[56]

Revelation 20 and the Biblical Picture of the Millennium

Revelation 20:1-10 stands at the center of all Christian discussion about the millennium:

> Then I saw an angel coming down from heaven, holding in his hand the key to the bottomless pit and a great chain. And he seized the dragon, that ancient serpent, who is the devil and Satan, and

bound him for a thousand years, and threw him into the pit, and shut it and sealed it over him, so that he might not deceive the nations any longer, until the thousand years were ended. After that he must be released for a little while.

Then I saw thrones, and seated on them were those to whom the authority to judge was committed. Also I saw the souls of those who had been beheaded for the testimony of Jesus and for the word of God, and those who had not worshiped the beast or its image and had not received its mark on their foreheads or their hands. They came to life and reigned with Christ for a thousand years. The rest of the dead did not come to life until the thousand years were ended. This is the first resurrection. Blessed and holy is the one who shares in the first resurrection! Over such the second death has no power, but they will be priests of God and of Christ, and they will reign with him for a thousand years. (Revelation 20:1-6)

John's vision portrays several key realities:

- Satan is bound so that he can no longer deceive the nations during the thousand years.
- The saints—especially those who suffered for Christ—"came to life and reigned with Christ" during this period.
- After the thousand years, Satan is released for a short time, instigates a final rebellion, and is then utterly defeated and cast into the lake of fire (Rev. 20:7-10).

The imagery of peace, justice, and righteous rule found in this vision echoes earlier Old Testament promises. Prophets such as Isaiah spoke of a coming age marked by harmony among the nations and the restoration of creation (Isa. 2:1-5; 11:1-9). Daniel envisioned a kingdom established by God Himself, one that would crush all human empires and endure forever (Dan. 2:44-45; 7:13-14,

27). These texts form the theological backdrop for John's apocalyptic vision of Christ's triumph.

The New Testament elsewhere affirms that Christ already reigns as the risen Lord, seated at the right hand of the Father (1 Cor. 15:22-25; Rev. 2:26-29). Revelation 20, then, does not introduce a new or separate kingship of Christ, but focuses attention on how His reign and the defeat of Satan unfold in relation to the final judgment and the new creation.[57] Different millennial views arise largely from different readings of this relationship.

Major Christian Views of the Millennium

Throughout the history of the church, faithful Christians have offered different answers to how Revelation 20 should be understood. Within conservative evangelicalism, these views are commonly grouped into three main positions: premillennialism, postmillennialism, and amillennialism. What follows is a descriptive summary of each, highlighting areas of agreement and difference while avoiding speculation beyond what Scripture clearly reveals.

Premillennialism

Premillennialism teaches that Jesus Christ will return *before* the millennium.[58] According to this view, Christ's second coming will inaugurate a literal or concrete reign on earth, lasting a thousand years (or a period symbolically represented by that number), after which the final judgment and eternal state will follow.

Historically, premillennialism appears to have been common among Christians in the first few centuries of the church.

Early figures such as Papias, Justin Martyr, Irenaeus, and Tertullian anticipated a future reign of Christ closely connected to Old Testament promises of restoration and the vindication of the martyrs.[59]

In the modern era, premillennialism diversified. Historic premillennialism emphasizes a post-tribulational return of Christ followed by His earthly reign. Dispensational premillennialism, associated with John Nelson Darby, C. I. Schofield, and later popular writers, often distinguishes more sharply between Israel and the church and commonly teaches a pre-tribulational rapture followed by the millennium.[60] While these forms differ, both share the conviction that Christ's visible return precedes a distinct millennial reign.

Many evangelical theologians who lean premillennial argue that this reading takes the sequence of Revelation 19-20 in a more straightforward way: Christ appears in glory (Rev. 19), defeats His enemies, and then reigns with His saints (Rev. 20:4-6) before the final judgment and new creation (Rev. 20:11-21:4). Others within the evangelical family, however, understand the same chapters symbolically and caution against building a detailed chronology from apocalyptic imagery.[61]

Postmillennialism

Postmillennialism teaches that Christ will return *after* the millennium. According to this view, the millennium represents a prolonged period—whether literal or symbolic—in which the gospel advances powerfully, transforms societies, increases righteousness, and extends the visible influence of Christ's reign throughout the world.

Elements of this perspective appeared early, but it developed more fully in the medieval and early modern periods. Theologians such as Daniel Whitby, and later some Reformed thinkers, emphasized the progressive triumph of the gospel in history. During the eighteenth and nineteenth centuries, postmillennialism contributed to a strong sense that missionary work, evangelism, and social reform were means by which God would bring about a period of widespread Christian influence before Christ's return.[62]

The traumatic events of the twentieth century—especially two world wars and global totalitarian regimes—led many Christians to question the strong historical optimism often associated with this view. As a result, postmillennialism declined in many circles, though it continues to be held by some within Reformed and evangelical traditions, often with a more cautious, biblically framed optimism about the long-term fruit of the Great Commission. [63]

Postmillennialists stress passages that speak of the nations coming to the Lord and of the growth of the kingdom, such as the Great Commission (Matt. 28:18-20), the leaven and the mustard seed (Matt. 13:31-33), and prophecies about the nations streaming to Zion (Isa. 2:1-4). Critics, including many evangelical theologians, caution that these texts do not specify a golden age prior to Christ's return and that the New Testament also speaks plainly of ongoing opposition and suffering until the end.

Amillennialism

Amillennialism holds that there will be no future, literal thousand-year reign of Christ on earth distinct from the final state. Instead, the millennium is understood symbolically as the present reign of Christ from heaven during the church age. According to this view, Satan's binding in Revelation 20 refers to the restriction of his power to deceive the nations in such a way as to prevent the spread of the gospel, and the reign of the saints occurs as believers share in Christ's authority now and enter His presence at death.

This perspective was developed by early Christian thinkers such as Origen and was given its most influential formulation by Augustine. Augustine's interpretation shaped the theology of the medieval church and was carried forward, with variations, by many Protestant Reformers.[64] In the modern period, amillennialism remains a dominant view within Eastern Orthodoxy, Roman Catholicism, and many Reformed and evangelical churches.

Amillennial interpreters emphasize the symbolic nature of Revelation's visions and the way the book presents cycles of judgment and triumph rather than a simple linear timeline.[65] They often see Revelation 20 as recapitulating the same period as Revelation 12-19 from a different angle, highlighting the present victory of Christ over Satan through the cross and resurrection.

Evangelicals who hold this view stress that the New Testament consistently presents Christ as reigning now and that believers already participate in His kingdom while awaiting His return. Those who differ from amillennialism agree that Christ presently reigns, but they see Revelation 20 as indicating an additional, more visible phase of that reign before the eternal state.[66]

Unity Amid Diversity

Despite real disagreements over the nature and timing of the millennium, all orthodox Christian views affirm several essential truths. Jesus Christ is the crucified and risen Lord. He reigns over history now. He will return bodily and gloriously. Evil will be decisively defeated, the dead will be raised, and God's purposes will be brought to completion.

Wayne Grudem, Millard Erickson, and other evangelical systematicians emphasize that these shared convictions form the heart of Christian eschatology, while millennial positions represent secondary, though important, differences among believers.[67] The millennium, however understood, serves to direct the church's attention to the certainty of Christ's victory rather than to speculative timelines. Properly approached, this doctrine encourages humility, faithfulness, and hope.

Conclusion

The doctrine of the millennium invites believers to reflect carefully on how Christ's reign relates to the unfolding of history. While Scripture allows for different interpretations regarding the details of Revelation 20, it speaks with clarity about the outcome: Christ will reign until all His enemies are put under His feet, and God will be all in all (1 Cor. 15:25-28).

Within that shared hope, Christians may differ on whether the thousand years of Revelation 20 describe a future earthly reign, a long period of gospel triumph before Christ's return, or the present church age viewed from heaven's perspective. What unites them is confidence that the risen Christ will complete the work He has begun, that His victory over Satan is certain, and that His people will share in His reign forever in the new heavens and the new earth.

Chapter 5

The Renewal of Creation:
The New Heavens and the New Earth

Introduction

The Bible's vision of the future is not an escape from creation but its restoration. When Scripture speaks of the "new heavens and the new earth," it presents the final goal of God's redemptive work: a renewed cosmos in which God dwells permanently with His redeemed people (Isa. 65:17; Rev. 21:1-3).[68] Far from being a purely spiritual or abstract hope, this promise points to the healing, renewal, and perfection of the created order itself.

This chapter surveys the biblical teaching on the new heavens and the new earth, tracing God's plan to redeem creation from its beginning in Genesis, through the prophetic hope of the Old Testament, to its fulfillment in Christ and final revelation in the book of Revelation. In doing so, it clarifies why the Christian hope is fundamentally *creational* and why eternal life is inseparable from the renewal of the world.

Defining the New Heavens and the New Earth

The new heavens and the new earth refer to the eschatologically renewed state of the cosmos following the final judgment, in which the effects of sin, death, and corruption are fully removed. Scripture teaches that this renewed creation will be the eternal dwelling place of all who belong to Christ (Isa. 66:22; Rev. 21:1-4).

> 'For as the new heavens and the new earth that I make shall remain before me,' says the Lord, 'so shall your offspring and your name remain.' (Isa. 66:22)

> Then I saw a new heaven and a new earth, for the first heaven and the first earth had passed away, and the sea was no more. (Rev. 21:1)

In Scripture, the word "new" often carries the sense of renewed or transformed rather than entirely replaced.[69] Evangelical theologians commonly note that, just as the believer's resurrection body is continuous with the present body yet gloriously changed, so the future creation will be continuous with it while being set free from decay and perfected according to God's purposes (1 Cor. 15:42-44).[70]

From a conservative evangelical perspective, the central affirmation is clear: God's final work includes the restoration of the created order, not its abandonment. The precise manner in which God brings about this transformation is not fully detailed in Scripture, and so should be approached with humility. What is explicit, however, is that the new creation will be both truly renewed and truly secure, enduring forever before the Lord (Isa. 66:22).

God's Purpose to Redeem Creation

From the opening chapters of Genesis, Scripture presents creation as good, ordered, and designed for fellowship between God and humanity (Gen. 1-2). Human beings are created in God's image and entrusted with the responsibility to exercise dominion under God's rule (Gen. 1:26-28). When Adam and Eve rebelled, the consequences of sin extended beyond human relationships to affect the entire created order. God declared that the ground itself was cursed because of human disobedience (Gen. 3:17).

The apostle Paul reflects on this reality when he writes that creation was "subjected to futility" and now exists in bondage to corruption (Rom. 8:20-21). The brokenness of the world—seen in suffering, disorder, and death—is not accidental, nor is it permanent. It is the result of sin, and it awaits redemption.

Crucially, God's saving purpose has always included the restoration of creation itself. Salvation is the rescue of individual souls and the renewal of the world God made. Paul describes creation as "groaning together in the pains of childbirth until now," and adds that believers "groan inwardly as we wait eagerly for adoption as sons, the redemption of our bodies" (Rom. 8:22-23). The hope of believers and the hope of creation are inseparably linked.[71]

Isaiah's Prophetic Vision of Renewal

Among the Old Testament prophets, Isaiah offers one of the clearest and most vivid portraits of the renewed creation. His visions portray a world transformed by God's righteous reign, where harmony replaces hostility and life flourishes without fear.

In Isaiah 11:6-8, the prophet describes a peace so comprehensive that even natural enmities within the animal world are overcome.

> The wolf shall dwell with the lamb,
> and the leopard shall lie with the young goat,
> and the calf and the lion and the fattened calf together;
> and a little child shall lead them.
>
> The cow and the bear shall graze;
> their young shall lie down together;
> and the lion shall eat straw like the ox.
>
> The nursing child shall play over the hole of the cobra,
> and the weaned child shall put his hand on the adder's den.
>
> They shall not hurt or destroy
> in all my holy mountain;
> for the earth shall be full of the knowledge of the Lord
> as the waters cover the sea. (Isa. 11:6-9)

Predators and prey coexist, and children live without danger. The imagery is poetic and symbolic, yet the theological message is plain: God's future entails the reversal of the curse and the restoration of creation to harmony under His reign.

Later, Isaiah speaks explicitly of "new heavens and a new earth" that will endure forever before the Lord (Isa. 66:22). In Isaiah 65:17-25, he describes long life, joy, fruitful labor, and the absence of tragedy. While the language is expressed through familiar categories drawn from the prophet's own time, the theological message is clear: God's future involves the renewal of embodied life within a restored world.

While interpreters differ on how much of this language refers to intermediate stages of God's work and how much to the final state, conservative evangelicals agree that Isaiah's vision points toward a renewed order in which God's people enjoy His blessing in a restored world.[72] The Old Testament hope is therefore not merely "going to heaven," but the comprehensive renewal of life under God's rule.[73]

New Creation and Fulfillment in Christ

By the time of the Second Temple period, Jewish expectation increasingly included both the resurrection of the dead and the renewal of creation (Dan. 12:2). The New Testament presents Jesus Christ as the fulfillment and guarantee of these hopes.

Christ's resurrection is the beginning of the new creation. Paul calls the risen Christ the "firstfruits" of those who will be raised (1 Cor. 15:20-23), indicating that His resurrection inaugurates the future renewal of all things. Jesus' authority over nature—seen in His calming of the storm and His healing miracles—further reveals His lordship over creation and anticipates its restoration.

This new-creation reality already touches believers in the present. Paul declares, "If anyone is in Christ, he is a new creation" (2 Cor. 5:17). Through union with Christ, believers participate now in the life of the age to come. Baptism signifies dying and rising with Christ (Rom. 6:3-5), and the indwelling Holy Spirit serves as a guarantee of future resurrection and renewal (2 Cor. 5:5).

Yet this participation remains partial. Believers still live in a broken world, awaiting the full transformation of their bodies and the world itself. The Spirit's presence is the down payment, assuring that what has begun will one day be completed.

The Final Vision in Revelation

The most comprehensive biblical picture of the new heavens and the new earth appears in Revelation 21-22. After the defeat of Satan and the final judgment (Rev. 20:10-15), John writes:

> Then I saw a new heaven and a new earth, for the first heaven and the first earth had passed away, and the sea was no more. And I saw the holy city, new Jerusalem, coming down out of heaven from God, prepared as a bride adorned for her husband. And I heard a loud voice from the throne saying, 'Behold, the dwelling place of God is with man. He will dwell with them, and they will be his people, and God himself will be with them as their God. He will wipe away every tear from their eyes, and death shall be no more, neither shall there be mourning, nor crying, nor pain anymore, for the former things have passed away.' (Rev. 21:1-4)

Several features stand out in this vision. First, heaven comes down to earth: the holy city descends "out of heaven from God," joining God's dwelling and human dwelling rather than replacing the earth altogether. Second, the central blessing is the unbroken presence of God with His people— "the dwelling place of God is with man." Third, all the consequences of sin—death, mourning, crying, and pain—are abolished. The curse that began in Genesis 3 is completely undone (Rev. 22:3).

John later notes that the glory of God and the Lamb fills the renewed creation with light: "And the city has no need of sun or moon to shine on it, for the glory of God gives it light, and its lamp is the Lamb" (Rev. 21:23). Evangelical interpreters differ on some details of the imagery—such as whether particular features of the city should be taken more literally or symbolically—but they agree on the main point: God will bring about a final order in which His presence, His people, and His renewed creation are united forever in righteousness and peace.[74]

Conclusion

The Bible begins with creation and ends with new creation. From Genesis to Revelation, God's redemptive plan encompasses both the salvation of sinners and the restoration of the world He made.[75] The curse of sin fractured both humanity and creation, but the saving work of Christ guarantees that one day all things will be made new.

The promise of the new heavens and the new earth reminds believers that eternity is not an escape from embodied life, but its fulfillment. The Christian hope is the hope of a renewed world—free from sin, suffering, and death—where God dwells with His people forever. This vision anchors faith, strengthens endurance, and directs hope toward the glorious future God has promised.

Part Three

Life Beyond Death

Chapter 6

Death and the Hope of Life Beyond the Grave

Introduction

When people think about life after death, they often imagine disembodied existence—souls floating in heaven, freed from the limitations of the physical world. Scripture presents a richer and more hopeful vision. God created human beings as embodied creatures, and His redemptive purpose includes not only the salvation of the soul but the resurrection and transformation of the body. Death, therefore, is not the end of the human story; it is a temporary rupture that will ultimately be overcome by God's power.

This chapter examines what Scripture teaches about life after death, focusing on the believer's immediate hope after death, the future resurrection of the body, and the certainty of eternal life through union with Christ. By integrating biblical teaching across both testaments, we will see that Christian hope is firmly grounded in the resurrection of Jesus and the promise that those who belong to Him will live forever in glorified bodies.[76]

Defining Life After Death

The doctrine of life after death describes what happens to human beings following physical death and explains the future resurrection and glorification of the body. Scripture teaches that human existence does not cease at death. Rather, death introduces a new phase in God's redemptive plan, one that culminates in resurrection and eternal life. Christian teaching affirms two essential truths: first, that believers who die are immediately in the presence of Christ; second, that this intermediate state, though blessed, is not the final goal. God's ultimate purpose is the resurrection of the body and full participation in the renewed creation (2 Cor. 5:1-5; Rom. 8:18-23). Conservative evangelical theologians regularly warn against viewing heaven as a permanent disembodied state; the biblical hope is resurrection life in a restored creation.[77]

Being with Christ After Death

The New Testament offers clear comfort regarding the state of believers after death. In Philippians 1, the apostle Paul reflects on his own mortality:

> For to me to live is Christ, and to die is gain. If I am to live in the flesh, that means fruitful labor for me. Yet which I shall choose I cannot tell. I am hard pressed between the two. My desire is to depart and be with Christ, for that is far better. (Phil. 1:21-23)

This passage indicates that when believers die, they are immediately "with Christ." Although the body returns to the ground, the believer is not unconscious or separated from the Lord (cf. 2 Cor. 5:6-8). Paul's confidence offers deep pastoral assurance:

death does not separate the Christian from Christ but brings the believer into closer fellowship with Him.[78]

At the same time, Paul's willingness to remain and serve the church shows that life on earth retains genuine purpose. The hope of being with Christ does not diminish present faithfulness; it strengthens it. Knowing that "to die is gain" frees believers to live sacrificially, without fear of death, because their future with Christ is secure.

It is important to be clear about what this hope does and does not mean. The New Testament does not present believers as entering a state of soul-sleep in which they are unaware of Christ, nor does it describe the intermediate state as the final form of Christian existence. Being "away from the body and at home with the Lord" (2 Cor. 5:8) is a conscious, blessed fellowship with Christ, yet it still looks forward to something greater—the day when body and soul are reunited in resurrection glory and believers share fully in the life of the renewed creation.

The Resurrection of the Body

While Scripture affirms conscious life with Christ after death, it places even greater emphasis on the future resurrection of the body. The most extensive biblical teaching on this subject appears in 1 Corinthians 15:

> So is it with the resurrection of the dead. What is sown is perishable; what is raised is imperishable. It is sown in dishonor; it is raised in glory. It is sown in weakness; it is raised in power. It is sown a natural body; it is raised a spiritual body. If there is a natural body, there is also a spiritual body. (1 Cor. 15:42-44)

Paul addresses common questions about how the dead are raised by using the image of a seed planted in the ground. What is buried appears weak and ordinary, yet what emerges is transformed by God's power. In the same way, the body that is "sown" perishable will be raised imperishable. It is sown in weakness and dishonor but raised in power and glory.

When Paul speaks of a "spiritual body," he does not mean a nonphysical or ghostlike existence. Rather, he describes a body fully animated and sustained by the Holy Spirit. The resurrected body will be truly physical, yet free from decay, sickness, and death (Phil. 3:20-21). Believers will bear the image of the risen Christ, the "man of heaven," just as they once bore the image of Adam, the "man of dust" (1 Cor. 15:49).[79]

Paul concludes this teaching with a triumphant declaration of victory:

> When the perishable puts on the imperishable, and the mortal puts on immortality, then shall come to pass the saying that is written: 'Death is swallowed up in victory,' 'O death, where is your victory? O death, where is your sting?' (1 Cor. 15:54-55)

The resurrection of the body marks the final defeat and the fulfillment of God's saving work. For this reason, the early church's confession centered not simply on "life after death" but on "the resurrection of the dead and the life of the world to come."

Resurrection, Judgment, and Eternal Life

Scripture teaches that resurrection is inseparably connected to judgment and eternal destiny. Jesus Himself declared that "all who are in the tombs will hear his voice and come out" (John 5:28-29). All will be raised; what distinguishes destinies is one's relationship to Christ, expressed in faith and obedience.[80]

For believers, resurrection is guaranteed through union with Christ. Romans 6:5-14 explains that those who have been united with Christ in His death will also share in His resurrection life. Because Christ has been raised never to die again, death no longer has dominion over those who are in Him (Rom. 6:9). Eternal life is not merely endless duration but restored, embodied fellowship with God in righteousness and joy.[81]

The New Testament also connects resurrection with the evaluation of believers' lives. Paul writes that "we must all appear before the judgment seat of Christ" (2 Cor. 5:10), and that "each one's work will become manifest" (1 Cor. 3:13). For those in Christ, this judgment does not threaten their salvation, which rests on Christ's finished work, but it does underscore the seriousness of discipleship. The same resurrection that brings comfort also brings accountability, assuring believers that their choices, sacrifices, and obedience in this life truly matter and will be brought into the light of Christ's righteous assessment.

The hope of resurrection extends beyond individual believers to the entire people of God. Hebrews concludes its survey of Old Testament saints by saying:

> And all these, though commended through their faith, did not receive what was promised, since God had provided something better for us, that apart from us they should not be made perfect. (Hebrews 11:39-40)

This reminds readers that the faithful of earlier generations await the same resurrection and perfection that New Testament believers await. Resurrection life is a shared inheritance, uniting the people of God across all ages.

Life in the Presence of God

The book of Revelation offers a vivid picture of the life that awaits God's redeemed people. In Revelation 7:9-10, John writes:

> After this I looked, and behold, a great multitude that no one could number, from every nation, from all tribes and peoples and languages, standing before the throne and before the Lamb, clothed in white robes, with palm branches in their hands, and crying out with a loud voice, 'Salvation belongs to our God who sits on the throne, and to the Lamb!' (Rev. 7:9-10)

This scene emphasizes both the diversity and unity of God's people and their shared joy in worship. John further describes their condition:

> They shall hunger no more, neither thirst anymore;
> the sun shall not strike them,
> nor any scorching heat.
>
> For the Lamb in the midst of the throne will be their shepherd,
> and he will guide them to springs of living water,
> and God will wipe away every tear from their eyes. (Rev. 7:16-17)

Those who stand before the throne are free from hunger, thirst, and suffering. God shelters them with His presence, and "the Lamb in the midst of the throne" shepherds them and leads them to springs of living water. This vision reinforces the truth that eternal life is communal, embodied, and centered on the presence of God. Heaven is not static or dull but filled with worship, fellowship, and joy, all flowing from the direct presence of the Lamb. [82]

A Note on Christian Traditions and the Intermediate State

All orthodox Christian traditions affirm life after death and the future resurrection of the body. Differences arise in how the intermediate state is understood and emphasized, reflecting broader theological commitments rather than disagreements about the authority of Scripture. Where Scripture speaks clearly, Christians may speak with confidence. Where Scripture is more reticent—about the precise conditions of the soul between death and resurrection, or the details of purification—wise theology proceeds with humility and restraint.

Roman Catholic Perspective

The Roman Catholic tradition affirms that believers who die in Christ continue in conscious existence and will one day experience bodily resurrection. Catholic theology also includes the doctrine of purgatory, understood as a temporary state of final purification for those who die in God's grace but still require cleansing from the effects of sin. It is not presented as a second chance for salvation, but as the completion of sanctification prior to the full enjoyment of God's presence. Catholics likewise emphasize the communion of saints and the unity of the church across death.

Eastern Orthodox Perspective

Eastern Orthodox theology strongly emphasizes resurrection and restoration. Death is viewed primarily as an unnatural intrusion into God's life. Orthodox writers typically speak with restraint about the intermediate state, stressing mystery more than detailed description. Heaven and hell are sometimes described in relational terms—as different experiences of the same divine presence—rather than as merely spatial locations.

Protestant (Reformation) Perspectives

Most Protestant traditions reject the doctrine of purgatory, affirming instead that believers are justified fully by faith in Christ and enter immediately into His presence at death. This conviction rests on texts such as Philippians 1:23 and 2 Corinthians 5:8, which emphasize being "with Christ" after death. Within Protestantism, there is broad agreement on conscious existence after death, bodily resurrection at Christ's return, final judgment, and eternal life with God. Differences tend to concern how best to describe the intermediate state, not whether it exists.[83]

Reformed and Presbyterian Traditions

Within Reformed theology, the intermediate state is often understood as a conscious, blessed communion with Christ, while resurrection—not disembodied heaven—is emphasized as the final goal. Classic Reformed confessions stress assurance, union with Christ, and the sovereignty of God in both salvation and judgment, and they caution against speculation beyond what Scripture reveals.

Baptist and Evangelical Traditions

Baptist and broader evangelical traditions generally affirm immediate, conscious presence with Christ after death for believers and bodily resurrection at the last day. Some evangelical discussions have raised the idea of "soul sleep"; however, this view has remained a minority position; the dominant evangelical emphasis aligns with what has been described in this chapter:

conscious fellowship with Christ after death and future resurrection in a glorified body. [84]

Areas of Shared Christian Agreement

Despite these differences, all orthodox Christian traditions affirm several foundational truths:

- Death does not end human existence.

- God will raise the dead bodily.

- Eternal destiny is determined by one's relation to Christ.

- Resurrection, not disembodied existence, is the ultimate hope.

- God's justice and mercy will be fully revealed.

These shared convictions form the core of Christian eschatological hope and provide unity amid interpretive diversity.[85]

Living in Light of the Resurrection

The doctrine of life after death is not given to satisfy curiosity about the future alone; it is meant to shape how Christians live in the present. Because believers share in Christ's death and resurrection, they are called to "consider [themselves] dead to sin and alive to God in Christ Jesus" (Rom. 6:11).

The certainty of resurrection encourages holiness, courage, and perseverance. Christians need not fear death or cling desperately to the temporary goods of this world. Instead, they are free to live generously and faithfully, confident that "your labor is not in vain in the Lord" (1 Cor. 15:58). A robust hope in the resurrection produces steadfastness in trials, willingness to suffer for Christ, and compassion for those who grieve, because death is seen not as the last word but as the doorway to the life that is truly life.[86]

Conclusion

The Bible's teaching on life after death centers on the resurrection of the body and eternal life with God. Believers who die are immediately with Christ, yet they await a greater hope—the resurrection and glorification of the body. This hope rests securely on the resurrection of Jesus, who has conquered death once and for all.

Christian eschatology therefore proclaims not escape from embodied existence, but its redemption.[87] Life after death is the promise that God will make His people whole, restoring them to eternal life in His presence and within His renewed creation. This hope, shared across the main streams of Christian orthodoxy and articulated with particular clarity in conservative evangelical theology, offers comfort in grief and strength for faithful living until the day when death is swallowed up in victory.

Chapter 7

Heaven

The Dwelling Place of God and the Hope of the Redeemed

Introduction

Few doctrines offer as much comfort and encouragement as the Christian hope of heaven. Scripture presents heaven not only as the place where God presently dwells in glory, but also as the promised home of all who belong to Jesus Christ. Reflection on heaven strengthens believers in suffering, shapes faithful living in the present, and fuels worship rooted in hope rather than fear.

This chapter examines the biblical teaching on heaven, paying close attention to the different ways Scripture uses the term and to the place of heaven within God's larger redemptive plan. Rather than treating heaven as an isolated topic, the Bible consistently presents it in relation to God's presence, Christ's reign, and the ultimate renewal of all things. Conservative evangelical voices remind us that the hope of heaven is inseparable from the hope of resurrection and the new creation; heaven is part of, not a substitute for, God's final purpose to dwell with His people forever.[88]

Defining Heaven in Scripture

The Bible refers to heaven as God's "holy habitation" (Deut. 26:15). It is the realm of God's throne, the sphere of His sovereign authority, and the present dwelling place of those who serve Him (Ps. 103:19; Heb. 12:22-24).[89] At the same time, heaven is also spoken of as the future home of the redeemed—a place of rest, joy, and communion with God.

Scripture uses the word *heaven* in several related but distinct ways. Recognizing these helps avoid confusion and allows the Bible's teaching to be understood with greater clarity.

Heaven as the Created Sky

In its most basic sense, *heaven* refers to the visible sky and the celestial realm. The opening verse of Scripture declares that God created "the heavens and the earth" (Gen. 1:1), referring to the expanse above the earth and the earthly sphere below. God set "the greater light to rule the day and the lesser light to rule the night— and the stars" (Gen. 1:16). Birds are said to fly "across the expanse of the heavens" (Gen. 1:20), and God promised Abraham that his descendants would be as numerous as "the stars of heaven" (Deut. 10:22).

This usage emphasizes God's creative power and the beauty of the ordered universe. It also provides the language by which Scripture points beyond the visible sky to a higher, unseen reality—the dwelling place of God.

Heaven as the Dwelling Place of God

Scripture frequently speaks of heaven as something higher than the physical sky—the place associated uniquely with God's presence. Angels speak "from heaven" (Gen. 22:11, 15), and God is repeatedly called "the God of heaven" (Gen. 24:3, 7; Neh. 1:5). Solomon acknowledges that even "heaven and the highest heaven cannot contain" God (1 Kings 8:27-30). Isaiah declares, "Thus says the Lord: 'Heaven is my throne, and the earth is my footstool'" (Isa. 66:1).

Moses prayed that God would "look down from your holy habitation, from heaven, and bless your people Israel" (Deut. 26:15), and the psalmist says, "The Lord looks down from heaven; he sees all the children of man" (Ps. 33:13). Jesus teaches His disciples to pray to "our Father in heaven" (Matt. 6:9), reinforcing heaven's association with God's authority, holiness, and care.

The earthly tabernacle and temple are described as "copies of the true things," while Christ has entered "into heaven itself, now to appear in the presence of God on our behalf" (Heb. 9:24). Heaven, therefore, is not merely a physical location within the universe but the transcendent, created realm where God's glory is fully manifest and from which He rules all things. [90]

Heaven as the Realm of Angels and Worship

Heaven is not depicted as empty or inactive. Scripture presents it as a place of continual worship and divine service. Jacob's dream revealed "a ladder set up on the earth, and the top of it reached to heaven" with "the angels of God…ascending and descending on it" (Gen. 28:12), signaling ongoing interaction between heaven and earth. The prophet Micaiah sees "the Lord sitting on his throne, and all the host of heaven standing beside him" (1 Kings 22:19).

Isaiah's vision of the Lord "sitting upon a throne, high and lifted up" includes seraphim crying, "Holy, holy, holy is the Lord of hosts; the whole earth is full of his glory!" (Isa. 6:1-3). In Revelation, John sees living creatures and elders around the throne, proclaiming, "Worthy is the Lamb who was slain" (Rev. 5:12). Heaven, then, is a dynamic realm where God is continually praised, and His will is joyfully carried out.[91]

Heaven as a Way of Speaking about God's Authority

At times, Scripture uses *heaven* as a reverent way of referring to God Himself and His sovereign rule. Daniel tells Nebuchadnezzar that his kingdom would be restored "when you know that Heaven rules" (Dan. 4:26), using "Heaven" as shorthand for God. Jesus asks whether John's baptism was "from heaven or from man" (Mark 11:30), referring to whether it came from God or merely from human origin.

This usage underscores the close connection between heaven and God's reign. To speak of heaven is often to speak of God's rule exercised in righteousness and power.

Heaven as the Present Home of the Redeemed

While the Old Testament offers only glimpses of heaven as the destiny of God's people, Jesus speaks of it plainly and often. He assured His followers that their reward is "great in heaven" (Matt. 5:12) and urges them to "lay up for yourselves treasures in heaven"

(Matt. 6:20). On the night before His crucifixion, Jesus comforts His disciples:

> In my Father's house are many rooms. If it were not so, would I have told you that I go to prepare a place for you? And if I go and prepare a place for you, I will come again and will take you to myself, that where I am you may be also. (John 14:2-3)

The New Testament repeatedly affirms that believers belong to heaven even now. Paul writes, "For we know that if the tent that is our earthly home is destroyed, we have a building from God, a house not made with hands, eternal in the heavens" (2 Cor. 5:1). He adds that "our citizenship is in heaven, and from it we await a Savior, the Lord Jesus Christ" (Phil. 3:20). Peter describes the believer's inheritance as "imperishable, undefiled, and unfading, kept in heaven for you" (1 Pet. 1:4).

These promises ground the Christian hope in a real and lasting future with God. When believers die, they enter the presence of Christ in heaven (Phil. 1:23; 2 Cor. 5:8), even as they await the resurrection of the body and the renewal of all things. Evangelical writers often describe this as "life after death," while the new heavens and new earth represent "life after life after death."[92]

Heaven as Rest and Meaningful Service

Heaven is described as a place of rest for God's people. The author of Hebrews speaks of a "Sabbath rest for the people of God" and urges believers to "strive to enter that rest" (Heb. 4:9-11). Yet this rest is not passivity or boredom. God's will is perfectly done in heaven (Matt. 6:10), and Scripture teaches that believers will share in Christ's rule.

Jesus' parables suggest that faithful servants will be entrusted with responsibility in the age to come: "And he said to him, 'Well done, good servant! Because you have been faithful in very little, you shall have authority over ten cities.'" (Luke 19:17)

Paul likewise writes, "If we endure, we will also reign with him" (2 Tim. 2:12). Revelation states that believers "will reign forever and ever" (Rev. 22:5). Heaven thus combines perfect peace with purposeful participation in God's rule. As many conservative evangelical pastors and theologians emphasize, heaven is a place of meaningful, joy-filled activity—worship, fellowship, service, and reigning with Christ—rather than an eternal idleness.[93]

Heaven and the New Heavens and the New Earth

The Bible ultimately directs attention beyond heaven understood only as "up there" to the final union of heaven and earth. God's redemptive plan is "to unite all things in [Christ], things in heaven and things on earth" (Eph. 1:10), and to "reconcile to himself all things, whether on earth or in heaven" (Col. 1:20).

This promise reaches its climax in Revelation 21:

> Then I saw a new heaven and a new earth, for the first heaven and the first earth had passed away, and the sea was no more. And I saw the holy city, new Jerusalem, coming down out of heaven from God… And I heard a loud voice from the throne saying, "Behold, the dwelling place of God is with man." (Rev. 21:1-3)

Here heaven is not abolished but comes down to earth; God's dwelling and humanity's dwelling are brought together. The storyline of Scripture moves from the separation of heaven and earth caused by sin (Gen. 3) to their eternal reunion through the saving work of Christ. Heaven, therefore, is not the final destination in isolation, but part of God's greater purpose to renew creation and dwell forever with His people.

Conservative evangelical theologians stress that the hope of heaven and the hope of the new earth are complementary, not competing: believers are with Christ in heaven after death, and ultimately they share in His presence in a renewed creation when heaven and earth are united.[94]

Heaven in Christian Theology

Throughout church history, orthodox Christian theology has consistently affirmed heaven as the dwelling place of God and the present home of believers who die in Christ. Classic confessions speak of souls of the righteous being "made perfect in holiness" and admitted into the presence of God, awaiting the resurrection of the body and the final judgment.

Within conservative evangelical circles, there is broad agreement on several key points: heaven is real; God reigns there in glory; believers are with Christ in heaven after death; and heaven is integrally connected to the final resurrection and the new creation. Differences in interpretation—such as how to picture heavenly rewards, what degree of continuity there is between present vocations and future service, and how to describe the relationship between heaven and the new earth—all reflect attempts to honor the biblical text rather than to deny its truth.[95]

The essential confession remains the same: heaven is the dwelling place of God, the present home of the redeemed who die in Christ, and a central part of God's eternal plan to gather His people and renew all things in His Son.

Conclusion

Heaven stands at the heart of Christian hope. It is the holy dwelling of God, the present home of the redeemed, and an essential dimension of God's plan to restore all things in Christ. Far from encouraging escapism, the promise of heaven strengthens faith, fuels holiness, and enables believers to endure suffering with confidence, knowing that "to be away from the body" is "to be at home with the Lord" (2 Cor. 5:8).[96]

Because heaven is real, life now is lived in light of eternity. Christians set their minds "on things that are above, where Christ is, seated at the right hand of God" (Col. 3:1), not to withdraw from earthly responsibilities but to engage them with hope-filled obedience. The Christian confession is simple and profound: heaven is home, heaven is promised, and in Christ, heaven is sure.

Chapter 8

Hell

Judgment, Separation, and the Justice of God

Introduction

The doctrine of hell is one of the most difficult and sobering teachings in Christian theology. It confronts readers with the reality of divine judgment, human accountability, and the eternal consequences of rejecting God's grace. For this reason, hell has often been misunderstood, minimized, or avoided altogether. Yet Scripture speaks of hell not to satisfy curiosity or inspire fear for its own sake, but to reveal the seriousness of sin, the holiness of God, and the urgency of repentance and faith. [97]

This chapter examines the biblical teaching of hell by tracing the language Scripture uses, the development of the concept within Jewish thought, the teaching of Jesus, and the consistent witness of the New Testament. In doing so, it seeks to present the doctrine with theological clarity and pastoral restraint, allowing Scripture to speak with both truth and gravity.

Defining Hell in Scripture

In biblical theology, hell refers to the final and eternal state of separation from God, experienced by those who persist in rejecting His saving grace in Christ. It is the condition in which God's righteous judgment is fully and irrevocably realized (Matt. 25:46; Rev. 20:11-15).[98]

While Scripture uses vivid imagery to describe hell, these images consistently communicate real judgment, conscious accountability, and permanence. Jesus speaks of "eternal punishment" in contrast to "eternal life" (Matt. 25:46), and Revelation describes those who oppose God as being tormented "day and night forever and ever" (Rev. 20:10). Hell is not a metaphor for earthly suffering, nor is it a temporary corrective state. It stands as the final outcome of impenitent rebellion against God.[99]

At the same time, Scripture does not satisfy every speculative question about the nature of hell. The biblical writers employ images of fire, darkness, exclusion, and destruction to communicate the horror of being finally separated from the gracious presence of God. Responsible theology recognizes the seriousness of these images without claiming to exhaust their mystery.

The Language of Hell:
Sheol, Hades, and Gehenna

Understanding the Bible's teaching on hell requires careful attention to the words Scripture uses and how their meaning develops across the canon.

Sheol in the Old Testament

In the Old Testament, the most common term associated with death is *Sheol*. Sheol refers broadly to the realm of the dead—the unseen place to which all people go after death (Deut. 32:22; Job 26:5-6; Ps. 88:3; Isa. 38:10). It is not initially presented as a place of punishment or reward, but as the shadowy domain of the dead, where both the righteous and the wicked are said to go.

Over time, however, Old Testament revelation reflects a growing awareness that Sheol cannot be the final word. The psalmist expresses confidence that God "will not abandon my soul to Sheol, or let your holy one see corruption" (Ps. 16:10). Daniel 12:2 anticipates a future resurrection in which "many of those who sleep in the dust of the earth shall awake, some to everlasting life, and some to shame and everlasting contempt." This development lays the foundation for later teaching about distinct eternal destinies and final judgment. [100]

Hades in Jewish and New Testament Thought

In the Greek translation of the Old Testament (the Septuagint), *Sheol* is most often translated as *Hades*. In the New Testament, Hades continues to denote the realm of the dead, particularly the temporary state between death and final judgment (Luke 16:23; Rev. 20:13).

Hades should not be equated directly with hell in its final sense. Revelation makes a clear distinction: at the final judgment, "Death and Hades were thrown into the lake of fire. This is the second death, the lake of fire" (Rev. 20:14). This indicates that Hades is temporary, whereas the lake of fire—the final state of judgment—is eternal.

Gehenna and Final Judgment

The most significant term for hell in the teaching of Jesus is *Gehenna*. Gehenna derives from the Valley of Hinnom, located outside Jerusalem, where child sacrifices were once offered in idolatrous worship (Jer. 7:31-32; 19:2-6). Because of its association with horrific sin and divine judgment, the valley became a powerful symbol in Jewish thought for God's final judgment.

By the time of Jesus, *Gehenna* had come to represent the ultimate destiny of the wicked. Jesus used this term deliberately to describe a final state of judgment characterized by exclusion from life and the presence of God. He warned of the danger of being thrown into "the hell of fire" (Matt. 5:22, 29-30), and spoke of Gehenna as a place "where their worm does not die and the fire is not quenched" (Mark 9:48). Unlike Sheol and *Hades*, Gehenna refers not to the realm of the dead in general, but to the irreversible outcome of divine judgment.[101]

Hell in the Teaching of Jesus

Jesus spoke about hell with striking clarity and frequency. He used images of fire, darkness, and exclusion—"The fiery furnace," "outer darkness," and "weeping and gnashing of teeth" (Matt. 8:12; 13:42, 50). These images communicate anguish, regret, and loss rather than mere physical pain.

Jesus taught that hell was originally prepared "for the devil and his angels" (Matt. 25:41), underscoring that it was not part of God's original design for humanity.[102] Yet He also warned that those who persist in rejecting God's reign place themselves under the same judgment. In the parable of the sheep and the goats, He declares that those who refuse to show mercy and respond to Him will "go away into eternal punishment, but the righteous into eternal life" (Matt. 25:46).

Significantly, Jesus' warnings about hell were always set within invitations to repentance and faith. He calls His hearers to "enter by the narrow gate" that leads to life (Matt. 7:13-14), promises rest to the weary and burdened (Matt. 11:28-30), and offers eternal life to all who believe in Him (John 3:16). Hell, in His teaching, serves not as a tool of manipulation but as a sober reminder of what is at stake in responding to God's grace.

The Witness of the New Testament

The New Testament consistently affirms the reality and seriousness of hell. Paul speaks of "the Lord Jesus…revealed from heaven with his mighty angels in flaming fire, inflicting vengeance on those who do not know God" and goes on to describe "the punishment of eternal destruction, away from the presence of the Lord and from the glory of his might" (2 Thess. 1:7-9). Here judgment is depicted as both punitive and relational: exclusion from the gracious presence of God.

Peter warns of "the day of judgment and destruction of the ungodly" (2 Pet. 3:7), and Jude refers to Sodom and Gomorrah as an example of those who "serve as an example by undergoing a punishment of eternal fire" (Jude 7).

The book of Revelation presents the most graphic imagery. John describes a "lake of fire" into which Satan, the beast, the false prophet, death, Hades, and those whose names are not found in the book of life are cast (Rev. 20:10, 14-15). He adds that "they will be tormented day and night forever and ever" (Rev. 20:10). While this language is apocalyptic and symbolic, its theological meaning is clear: God's final judgment is real, decisive, and everlasting.

Within conservative evangelical theology, these passages are taken to affirm a conscious, eternal judgment rather than temporary purification and eventual annihilation, even while recognizing that the precise nature of this experience is known only to God.[103]

Christian Interpretations of Hell

Throughout church history, Christians have agreed on the reality of eternal judgment while differing on how to interpret its imagery and how best to articulate its nature.

Roman Catholic theology historically emphasized hell as a state of definitive self-exclusion from communion with God by one's own free choice, in which the soul suffers the "pain of loss" (separation from God) and, traditionally, the "pain of sense," often described with the imagery of fire.

Eastern Orthodox theology often emphasizes hell as the experience of God's presence by those who reject His love. In this view, the same divine presence that brings joy to the righteous becomes a source of torment to the unrepentant, because they encounter God without reconciliation and without love.

Protestant theology generally affirms hell as an eternal reality grounded in Scripture, while allowing for symbolic interpretation of fire, darkness, and other images. A minority of Protestant theologians have argued for annihilationism—the view that the wicked are ultimately destroyed and cease to exist rather than enduring eternal conscious punishment. While this position appeals to texts that speak of "destruction" or "perishing," it remains a minority view within historic Christianity, and many conservative evangelicals contend that the parallel between "eternal punishment" and "eternal life" in Matthew 25:46 points toward an ongoing reality in both cases.[104]

Despite these differences, all orthodox traditions affirm that hell is real, that judgment is final, and that God's justice is inseparable from His holiness. Responsible Christian teaching on hell seeks to affirm what Scripture clearly reveals while resisting the temptation either to soften or to go beyond the biblical witness.

What the Doctrine of Hell Reveals

The doctrine of hell reveals the seriousness of sin and the moral weight of human choice. It affirms that God's justice is not arbitrary but righteous, measured, and necessary, flowing directly from His holy character (Rom. 2:5-6). Scripture consistently presents hell as a real and eternal judgment, not a temporary condition or symbolic abstraction. From a conservative evangelical perspective, hell represents the everlasting separation of the unrepentant from the gracious presence of God, a judgment that is conscious, just, and final (Matt. 25:46; Rev. 20:14-15).[105]

At the same time, the reality of hell magnifies the depth of God's mercy. The gospel proclaims that Christ willingly bore the judgment sinners deserve, satisfying divine justice through His atoning death so that salvation might be freely offered to all who believe (Isa. 53:5-6; 2 Cor. 5:21; Rom. 3:24-26; John 3:16-18). Hell, therefore, stands as a solemn witness to the costliness of grace and the seriousness of rejecting it.[106]

This doctrine also gives urgency to the church's mission. If eternal destinies are real and final, then proclamation of the gospel, faithful discipleship, and compassionate witness carry eternal significance. The teaching of hell presses the church toward kingdom-minded faithfulness, calling believers to speak the truth in love and to bear witness to Christ, who alone delivers from the judgment to come (Matt. 28:18-20; Rom. 10:13-15; 1 Thess. 1:9-10).[107]

Finally, the doctrine of hell safeguards the goodness of God's universe. It declares that evil will not have the last word, that unrepentant wickedness will not go unanswered, and that God will truly "judge the world in righteousness" (Acts 17:31). In this way, the reality of judgment is part of the Christian's confidence that God will set all things right.

Conclusion

The Bible's teaching on hell is sobering, but it is not devoid of hope. Hell stands as the tragic alternative to the life God offers in Christ, underscoring both the depth of human rebellion and the greatness of divine grace. Scripture presents judgment not as God's desire, but as the necessary outcome of persistent rejection of His love: He is "not wishing that any should perish, but that all should reach repentance" (2 Pet. 3:9), yet He will not forever ignore unrepentant evil.[108]

In Christian theology, hell serves as a solemn backdrop to the gospel. It reminds believers of the costliness of redemption, the urgency of faith, and the immeasurable mercy of God, who "so loved the world, that he gave his only Son" (John 3:16). To preach the good news faithfully is to speak honestly about both judgment and grace, calling all people to flee from the wrath to come and to find life in the crucified and risen Christ.

Chapter 9

The Fate of the Unevangelized

Introduction

Few questions in Christian theology provoke as much emotional weight and pastoral concern as the fate of the unevangelized. Believers across history have asked how God's justice and mercy relate to the reality that many people live and die without ever hearing the name of Jesus Christ. The question is not abstract. It touches grief for lost loved ones, urgency for missions, and confidence in the goodness of God.

Scripture does not address the issue by satisfying every curiosity, but neither does it leave the church without guidance. The Bible speaks clearly about God's self-revelation, the uniqueness of Christ, and humanity's accountability before God. At the same time, it consistently affirms that God judges with perfect righteousness and mercy. This chapter seeks to hold those truths together without speculation, sentimentality, or evasion.[109]

Defining the Question

The doctrine of the fate of the unevangelized addresses the eternal destiny of those who remain ignorant of the saving work of

Jesus Christ during their earthly lives. At its core, the question asks whether salvation is possible apart from explicit knowledge of the gospel and, if so, by what means.

This doctrine does not question whether Christ is the Savior of the world. Scripture is unambiguous on that point. Rather, it asks how the saving work of Christ relates to those who have never encountered the gospel message. Any faithful answer must therefore remain anchored in what Scripture clearly teaches while exercising humility where God has not spoken directly.

God's Revelation and Human Accountability

The apostle Paul provides the most sustained biblical reflection on this issue in Romans 1-2. In Romans 1:18-20, Paul teaches that God has revealed Himself to all people through creation:

> For what can be known about God is plain to them, because God has shown it to them. For his invisible attributes, namely, his eternal power and divine nature, have been clearly perceived, ever since the creation of the world, in the things that have been made. So they are without excuse. (Rom. 1:19-20)

The natural world bears witness to God's eternal power and divine nature, rendering humanity "without excuse." This form of revelation—often called *general revelation*—establishes human accountability before God.[110]

Paul continues in Romans 2:12-16 by explaining that Gentiles, though lacking the written Law, nonetheless possess a moral awareness that reflects God's righteous standards. Their consciences alternately accuse or excuse them, demonstrating that "the work of the law is written on their hearts" (Rom. 2:15).

Together, these passages affirm two essential truths: God has not left Himself without witness, and all people are responsible for how they respond to the light they are given. At the same time, Paul never suggests that general revelation provides a sufficient means of salvation. It reveals God's existence and moral will, but it does not reveal the saving work of Christ or the message of the cross.[111]

The Uniqueness of Christ

Any discussion of the unevangelized must be shaped by Scripture's clear teaching on the exclusivity of Christ. Jesus Himself declared, "I am the way, and the truth, and the life. No one comes to the Father except through me" (John 14:6). Peter proclaimed before the Sanhedrin that "there is salvation in no one else, for there is no other name under heaven given among men by which we must be saved" (Acts 4:12). Paul writes that "there is one God, and there is one mediator between God and men, the man Christ Jesus" (1 Tim. 2:5).

These texts establish that salvation is found only in Christ. He alone is the mediator between God and humanity, and His atoning work is the sole basis upon which anyone is saved.[112] The question, therefore, is not whether Christ saves, but whether His saving work may be applied to individuals who lack conscious knowledge of Him.

Major Christian Perspectives

Across Christian history, theologians have offered several responses to this question. These perspectives can be arranged along a spectrum, ranging from strict exclusivism to outright relativism. What follows is a descriptive summary, with evaluation guided by Scripture.

Ecclesiocentrism (Church-Centered View)

Ecclesiocentrism holds that salvation comes only through explicit faith in Jesus Christ and incorporation into His church. This view understands the church and the preached gospel as the ordained means by which God brings people into saving relationship with Christ.

Advocates emphasize texts such as Romans 10:13-17, which connect salvation to hearing and believing the gospel. They affirm that while all people are accountable for general revelation, salvation requires conscious repentance and faith in Christ. Variations of this view have been widely held within historic Christianity and remain common among conservative Roman Catholic, Reformed, and Baptist theologians.[113]

Agnosticism (Acknowledging the Limits of Revelation)

The agnostic approach maintains that Scripture does not provide sufficient detail to allow definitive conclusions about the eternal fate of every unevangelized person. Proponents of this view affirm Christ's uniqueness and the necessity of evangelism while emphasizing the mystery of God's mercy and justice.

Agnosticism may take a pessimistic form, assuming that most of the unevangelized are lost, or a more hopeful form, trusting that God's mercy may extend further than we can specify. This view appeals to texts that stress God's goodness and fairness (Gen. 18:25; Rom. 2:5-11), but it is often criticized for offering little concrete guidance beyond general affirmations of God's character.

Accessibilism (Response to General Revelation)

Accessibilism proposes that God may apply the saving work of Christ to individuals who respond faithfully to the limited revelation available to them through creation and conscience. According to this view, such individuals are saved by Christ alone, even though they do not know Him by name.

This position seeks to preserve both God's justice and mercy while continuing to affirm the necessity of Christ's atonement. Accessibilists often appeal to texts such as Romans 2:14-16 and Hebrews 11:6, where God commends faith that precedes full revelation. They argue that God may count such faith as a response to Christ, whom the person does not yet know explicitly. Critics respond that Scripture nowhere explicitly teaches salvation apart from hearing the gospel, and they warn against building doctrine from what the text does not clearly say.[114]

Religious Instrumentalism (Other Religions as Partial Means)

Religious instrumentalism suggests that other religions may function as partial or preparatory means through which God works saving grace. While Jesus remains the ultimate Savior, other religious traditions are seen as valid pathways toward God, containing elements that the Spirit might use to lead people to salvation.

This view attempts to honor religious diversity and God's universal work in the world, but it stretches beyond the bounds of biblical teaching. Scripture consistently presents salvation as grounded in the person and work of Christ and calls idolatry and false worship to repentance rather than recognizing other religions as parallel saving paths (Acts 17:29-31; 1 Thess. 1:9-10).[115]

Relativism (Many Paths to the Same God)

Relativism rejects the uniqueness of Christ altogether, asserting that all religions are equally valid paths to the same ultimate reality. Jesus is reduced to a moral teacher rather than the crucified and risen Lord, and evangelism is viewed as unnecessary or harmful.

This perspective stands wholly outside historic Christian orthodoxy. It directly contradicts the biblical witness to Christ's exclusive role as Savior and undermines the gospel's central claims.[116]

Theological and Pastoral Reflection

At the heart of this doctrine lies the tension between God's justice and God's mercy. Scripture affirms both without compromise. God reveals Himself to all people and holds them accountable, yet He has chosen to make salvation fully and finally known in Jesus Christ.

Several principles emerge from the biblical material:

- God's revelation is real and universal. No one is left without witness to God's existence and moral will (Rom. 1:19-20; Acts 14:17).

- Human sin is pervasive. All have sinned and fall short of the glory of God (Rom. 3:23); rejection of the light given is a universal reality apart from grace.

- Christ's work is sufficient and necessary. There is no salvation apart from His atoning death and resurrection, whether people lived before or after His earthly ministry (Rom. 3:24-26; Heb. 9:15).

- The ordinary means of salvation is the preached gospel. Faith ordinarily comes by hearing, and hearing through the word of Christ (Rom. 10:13-17).[117]

Within these boundaries, Scripture leaves some questions unanswered. It does not give a detailed map of every possible scenario concerning those who die without hearing the gospel. Wise theology acknowledges this limited knowledge, avoids dogmatic claims where Scripture is silent, and refuses to let theoretical possibilities blunt the clear biblical mandate for mission.

A Confessional Evangelical Affirmation

From a conservative evangelical and Baptist perspective, Scripture teaches that salvation is found only through the person and work of Jesus Christ, the sole mediator between God and humanity (John 14:6; Acts 4:12; 1 Tim. 2:5). General revelation is sufficient to render humanity accountable but insufficient to save; the gospel alone is "the power of God for salvation to everyone who believes" (Rom. 1:16).

This perspective affirms that:

- All who are saved—whether they have heard the gospel in this life or not—are saved only on the basis of Christ's atoning work.

- The normal pattern revealed in Scripture is that people come to saving faith through hearing and believing the message of Christ.[118]

- Scripture does not explicitly teach a separate category of people who are saved without any contact with the gospel; therefore, the church should not build its hope for the unevangelized on hypothetical exceptions but on God's revealed way of salvation.[119]

At the same time, evangelicals gladly confess that God is perfectly just and merciful, that He does what is right in every case (Gen. 18:25), and that His judgments are beyond full human comprehension (Rom. 11:33-36). We can trust that the Judge of all the earth will do right, even where we lack detailed knowledge.

The doctrine of the fate of the unevangelized, therefore, does not lessen the urgency of the church's mission—it intensifies it.[120] If people are lost apart from Christ, then the proper response is not speculation but obedience: proclaiming the gospel, supporting missions, and praying earnestly that all peoples may hear and respond to the saving message of Jesus Christ (Matt. 28:18-20; Rom. 10:13-15).

Conclusion

The Bible does not invite believers to resolve every tension surrounding the fate of the unevangelized. Instead, it calls the church to trust God's character, proclaim Christ faithfully, and rest in the assurance that the Judge of all the earth will do what is right.[121] God has made Himself known in creation and conscience, has revealed His saving grace in Jesus Christ, and has entrusted the gospel to His people for the life of the world.

This doctrine directs hearts toward mission, humility, and hope. It reminds believers that eternity is at stake in the church's witness and that the mercy of God revealed in Christ is sufficient for all who come to Him in faith.

Part Four

The Return of Christ

Chapter 10

The Second Coming of Jesus Christ

Introduction

From the earliest days of the church, Christians have confessed their hope in the return of Jesus Christ. This confession is woven into the fabric of the New Testament and into the worship of the church across the centuries. The Second Coming is not a peripheral belief, nor is it a subject reserved for speculation or fear. It is the climactic promise that the risen and ascended Christ will return to complete the work He has begun—to judge the world in righteousness, to raise the dead, and to bring the kingdom of God to its fullness (Acts 17:31; Rev. 11:15).[122]

For believers, the return of Christ is the moment when faith becomes sight and hope is fulfilled. This chapter examines the biblical teaching on the Second Coming with care and restraint, emphasizing what Scripture clearly affirms while resisting unnecessary conjecture.[123] The goal is to attend carefully to the meaning, certainty, and pastoral significance of Christ's promised return, as Scripture presents it to the church.

Defining the Second Coming

The doctrine of the Second Coming teaches that Jesus Christ will return bodily and visibly at the end of this age. His coming will bring final judgment upon the world and complete the establishment of His eternal kingdom. This return is a real historical event in which the same Jesus who was crucified, raised, and ascended will appear again in glory (Acts 1:9-11).

The New Testament frequently uses the Greek term *parousia*, meaning "arrival" or "presence," to describe this event (Matt. 24:3; 1 Thess. 4:15; 2 Thess. 2:1). The word emphasizes both the reality and the authority of Christ's return. The One who came first in humility will come again in power, not to suffer, but to reign (Phil. 2:9-11). Conservative evangelical theology stresses that this coming is personal, visible, and once-for-all, rather than a merely spiritual process or recurring experience.[124]

The Certainty and Mystery of Christ's Return

Jesus Himself taught clearly that His return would be certain, yet its timing would remain hidden. In Matthew 24:36, He declares, "But concerning the day and hour no one knows, not even the angels of heaven, nor the Son, but the Father only." When His disciples pressed Him for further details, Jesus consistently redirected their attention away from calculation and toward faithful readiness (Matt. 24:42-44).

This pattern appears again after the resurrection. In Acts 1:6-7, the disciples ask the risen Christ, "Lord, will you at this time restore the kingdom of Israel?" Their question reveals a sincere desire to understand the timing and shape of God's final work. Jesus did not rebuke the hope itself. Instead, He clarifies their calling: "It is not for you to know the times or seasons that the Father has fixed by his own authority" (Acts 1:7). The mystery remained, but their mission was made clear: "You will be my witnesses" (Acts 1:8).

These moments show that the mystery surrounding Christ's return is not accidental or temporary. God reveals the certainty of the event while withholding the schedule. This ordering protects the church from distraction and anchors faith in trust rather than control. In the language often used by evangelical scholars, believers are called to live in the tension of the "already and not yet" — Christ already reigns, yet His reign has not yet been revealed in its final fullness.[125]

By keeping the timing hidden, Jesus calls His followers in every generation to live in watchfulness and obedience. The Second Coming is presented as a promise to be trusted, calling believers to faithful readiness in every age (Titus 2:11-13).

The Nature of the Second Coming

While Scripture refrains from giving a detailed chronology, it speaks clearly about the character of Christ's return. During His trial, Jesus told the high priest, "You will see the Son of Man seated at the right hand of Power, and coming with the clouds of heaven" (Mark 14:62), echoing the vision of Daniel 7:13-14. His return will be public, visible, and unmistakable.

At the ascension, angels affirmed this same truth: "This Jesus, who has been taken from you into heaven, will come back in the same way you have seen Him go into heaven" (Acts 1:11). The return of Christ will correspond to His ascension—bodily, personal, and glorious.

Jesus Himself describes His coming as sudden and universal, likening it to lightning that flashes across the sky (Matt. 24:27). Paul speaks of "the revelation of the Lord Jesus from heaven with his mighty angels" (2 Thess. 1:7) and of Christ being "glorified in his saints" and "marveled at among all who have believed" (2 Thess. 1:10). Scripture leaves unanswered the question of how, in physical terms, every eye will see Him, but it leaves no doubt that His return will not be hidden or localized.[126] It will mark the decisive turning point of history, the unveiling of the King who already reigns.

Resurrection, Judgment, and the Kingdom

The Second Coming of Christ is inseparably connected to resurrection and judgment. Paul explains in 1 Thessalonians 4:16-17:

> For the Lord himself will descend from heaven with a cry of command, with the voice of an archangel, and with the sound of the trumpet of God. And the dead in Christ will rise first. Then we who are alive, who are left, will be caught up together with them in the clouds to meet the Lord in the air, and so we will always be with the Lord.

This passage offers comfort to grieving believers by affirming that death does not have the final word and that all who are in Christ—living or dead—will be gathered to Him.

In 1 Corinthians 15, Paul places the return of Christ within the larger story of God's kingdom:

> For as in Adam all die, so also in Christ shall all be made alive. But each in his own order: Christ the firstfruits, then at his coming those who belong to Christ. Then comes the end, when he delivers the

kingdom to God the Father after destroying every rule and every authority and power" (1 Cor. 15:22-24).

Christ, the firstfruits of the resurrection, will reign until every enemy—including death itself—has been defeated (1 Cor. 15:25-26). At His coming, believers will be transformed, and mortality will be swallowed up by life (1 Cor. 15:50-57; Phil. 3:20-21).

The New Testament also connects Christ's return with final judgment. Paul declares that God "has fixed a day on which he will judge the world in righteousness by a man whom he has appointed," giving assurance of this by raising Him from the dead (Acts 17:31). Jesus speaks of the Son of Man separating the nations as a shepherd separates sheep from goats (Matt. 25:31-46). Thus, the Second Coming does not introduce a new plan but completes God's redemptive purpose. It brings judgment upon evil, vindication for the righteous, and the final manifestation of Christ's reign over all things.[127]

The Expectation of the Church

The early church lived with a vivid expectation of Christ's return. Believers greeted one another with the prayer "Maranatha"—"Our Lord, come!" (1 Cor. 16:22). This expectancy shaped daily life, forming communities marked by holiness, endurance, and bold witness (1 Thess. 1:9-10; 2 Pet. 3:11-14).[128] Christians understood themselves to be living between Christ's first coming and His second, called to faithfulness as they awaited the fulfillment of God's promises.

Across the centuries, believers have reflected on world events in light of this hope. Scripture addresses this impulse by directing the church toward discernment, patience, and trust. Jesus warns against false alarms and false messiahs (Matt. 24:23-26) and calls His followers to sobriety and alertness: "Therefore you also must be ready, for the Son of Man is coming at an hour you do not expect" (Matt. 24:44). Paul echoes this when he says that the day of the Lord will come "like a thief in the night," yet believers are "not in darkness" so that this day should surprise them like a thief (1 Thess. 5:2-4).

The worship of the church continually renews this expectation. Each celebration of the Lord's Supper proclaims "the Lord's death until he comes" (1 Cor. 11:26). In this act of remembrance and anticipation, the church confesses that Christ's return belongs to the heart of its faith and hope, shaping its life until the day He appears.

Pastoral Significance of the Second Coming

The doctrine of the Second Coming nurtures confidence, hope, and perseverance in the life of the church. It assures believers that history moves toward God's appointed goal and that the risen Christ actively governs all things as they move toward completion (Eph. 1:20-22). Christ's return brings justice for the oppressed, rest for the weary, and renewal for a creation marked by suffering (2 Thess. 1:5-10; Rom. 8:18-25).[129]

This hope shapes the Christian life in the present. Believers are called to live "self-controlled and sober-minded" in light of "the end of all things" (1 Pet. 4:7). Expectation of Christ's return fosters active obedience marked by watchfulness, service, endurance, and joy (Matt. 24:45-47; 1 Cor. 15:58).[130] Knowing that the Lord will return to set all things right frees Christians from despair and fuels steadfast, hopeful labor in the Lord.

Each passing day draws the church nearer to the fulfillment of God's promises. The Second Coming directs believers to the reign of the risen Christ, who rules now and will one day be revealed openly as Lord of all. Until that day, the church waits with confidence, grounded in the faithfulness of the One who promised and who will surely come (Heb. 10:23; Rev. 22:20).

Conclusion

The Second Coming of Jesus Christ stands at the center of Christian hope. It proclaims that the story of redemption will not remain unfinished and that the crucified and risen Lord will return in glory. While Scripture calls believers to humility regarding the details, it calls them to certainty regarding the promise.[131]

Christ will come again. He will judge in righteousness, raise the dead, and bring the kingdom of God to its appointed completion. For those who belong to Him, this promise serves as a foundation of faith and a summons to live in holiness, hope, and patient endurance until the day He appears.

Chapter 11

The Rapture:
Interpretations and Implications

Introduction

Among the doctrines associated with the return of Christ, few have generated as much discussion as the rapture. For many Christians, the subject evokes questions about timing, sequence, and the relationship between Christ's return, the resurrection of the dead, and the culmination of history. Scripture speaks clearly about the gathering of believers to Christ, yet it does so with restraint, leaving room for faithful interpretation rather than definitive timelines.

This chapter seeks to present the biblical teaching related to the rapture with clarity and balance. Its purpose is not to press the reader toward a single interpretive conclusion, but to explain the major viewpoints that have emerged within orthodox Christianity. By examining the relevant texts and theological assumptions behind each position, readers are equipped to think carefully, remain rooted in Scripture, and hold their convictions with humility.[132]

Defining the Rapture

The term *rapture* comes from the Latin word *rapiemur*, used in the Latin translation of 1 Thessalonians 4:17, where believers are described as being "caught up" to meet the Lord in the air. English translations render this phrase as "caught up" or "snatched up." While the word *rapture* itself does not appear in Scripture, the language of being gathered to Christ at His coming clearly does.[133]

Biblically understood, the rapture refers to the gathering of living believers to Jesus Christ at the time of His return. This event is closely connected to the resurrection of the dead, the public appearing of Christ, and the completion of God's redemptive purposes. Disagreements among Christians do not concern whether believers will be gathered to Christ, but how this gathering relates to other end-time events.[134]

Key Biblical Texts

The most explicit New Testament passage associated with the rapture is 1 Thessalonians 4:13-18. Paul addresses believers who grieve the death of fellow Christians and writes:

> For the Lord himself will descend from heaven with a cry of command, with the voice of an archangel, and with the sound of the trumpet of God. And the dead in Christ will rise first. Then we who are alive, who are left, will be caught up together with them in the clouds to meet the Lord in the air, and so we will always be with the Lord. Therefore encourage one another with these words. (1 Thess. 4:16-18)

Here the emphasis falls on resurrection, reunion, and comfort. The Lord descends, the dead are raised, the living are transformed and caught up, and all are together with Christ forever. The passage does not explicitly specify how this event relates to tribulation or the millennium, which is why differing views arise.[135]

Other passages contribute to the broader framework. Jesus' discourse in Matthew 24 describes His coming with cosmic signs, the sounding of a trumpet, and the gathering of His elect "from the four winds" (Matt. 24:29-31). Paul speaks of believers being changed "in a moment, in the twinkling of an eye, at the last trumpet" (1 Cor. 15:51-52). Revelation 19-20 portrays Christ's victorious return and the final defeat of His enemies. These texts provide the context within which the doctrine of the rapture is discussed, even when they do not mention the "catching up" directly.[136]

Major Interpretive Approaches

Christian interpretations of the rapture differ primarily in how they understand its timing and relationship to tribulation, resurrection, and the millennial reign of Christ. These views arise from sincere attempts to read Scripture faithfully and to harmonize its teaching.

Premillennial Perspectives

Premillennial interpretations affirm that Christ will return before the establishment of His millennial reign. Within this framework, the rapture is closely connected to the resurrection of believers and the visible return of Christ, but its precise timing relative to a period of tribulation is debated.

Premillennial Christians hold several positions:

- Pre-tribulation views understand the gathering of believers to occur before a period of intense tribulation described in

Scripture. Believers are caught up to be with Christ, spared from the worst of end-time judgments, and then later return with Him in glory.

- Mid-tribulation or pre-wrath views place the rapture during the tribulation, often near its midpoint or just before the outpouring of God's final wrath, seeking to balance texts that speak of both suffering and deliverance.

- Post-tribulation views understand the rapture to occur at the conclusion of tribulation, immediately preceding Christ's public return and reign. Believers are caught up to meet Christ as He descends and then accompany Him in His victorious coming.

These interpretations often read prophetic texts in a more chronological sequence and, especially in dispensational forms, emphasize a distinction between Israel and the church.[137] While differing on timing, all premillennial views affirm the bodily return of Christ, the future resurrection of believers, and the certainty that Christ will ultimately reign.[138]

Amillennial Perspectives

Amillennial interpretations understand the rapture as part of a single, climactic return of Christ at the end of the present age. In this view, the "thousand years" of Revelation 20 symbolizes the current reign of Christ from heaven, and the rapture coincides with His visible appearing, the general resurrection, and the final judgment.

A key feature of this view involves the language of "meeting" in 1 Thessalonians 4:17. In the ancient world, the term was commonly used for citizens going out to greet a returning king and then accompanying him back into the city. From this perspective, the rapture depicts the church welcoming Christ and joining Him as He brings history to its appointed fulfillment, rather than being removed from the earth for an extended period.

This approach emphasizes continuity between Christ's return, the resurrection, the final judgment, and the renewal of heaven and earth, treating them as interconnected aspects of one decisive event (2 Pet. 3:10-13).[139]

Postmillennial Perspectives

Postmillennial interpretations understand Christ's return to follow an extended period of gospel advance, during which righteousness and peace increasingly shape the world. Within this framework, the rapture occurs at the conclusion of history, following the tribulation and coinciding with the resurrection of the righteous and final judgment.

Postmillennialists highlight the triumph of Christ's kingdom through the spread of the gospel and see the gathering of believers as the culmination of God's redemptive work in history.[140] The rapture, in this understanding, gathers the people of God to meet the returning King as He brings the present age to completion and ushers in the new heavens and new earth.

Points of Agreement

Despite differing interpretations, Christians across orthodox traditions share several essential convictions about the rapture and Christ's return:

1. Jesus Christ will return personally, bodily, and gloriously.

2. Believers will be gathered to Him and united with Him forever.

3. The resurrection of the dead, the final judgment, and the consummation of God's kingdom will accompany or follow His coming.

These shared affirmations form the doctrinal center of Christian hope and provide a foundation for charitable dialogue among believers, even as they differ over questions of timing and sequence.[141]

Pastoral Implications

The doctrine of the rapture serves a primary pastoral purpose. Paul concludes his teaching in 1 Thessalonians 4 with the exhortation, "Therefore encourage one another with these words" (1 Thess. 4:18). The promise of being gathered to Christ assures believers that neither death nor history itself can separate them from the Lord (cf. Rom. 8:38-39).[142]

This hope shapes Christian living in the present. Expectation of Christ's return—whatever one's precise rapture view—cultivates readiness, holiness, and perseverance (1 Thess. 5:4-8). It directs believers to live attentively, to serve with purpose, and to bear witness with confidence, knowing that the risen Christ will gather His people and complete His work.

At the same time, the variety of rapture interpretations invites humility. Scripture gives clear promises but limited detail. Wise pastoral teaching encourages believers to hold central truths firmly while showing charity toward brothers and sisters who differ in secondary matters of eschatological sequence.[143]

Conclusion

The doctrine of the rapture invites careful study, humble reflection, and faithful trust. Scripture affirms the gathering of believers to Christ when He returns, while allowing room for differing interpretations regarding its timing and relationship to tribulation and the millennium.[144] Rather than pressing for certainty where Scripture speaks with reserve, the church holds fast to what is clearly promised.

Christ will return, and His people will be gathered to Him. This assurance sustains the church across generations, calling believers to live with hope, readiness, and confidence as they await the appearing of their Lord.

Chapter 12

The Tribulation and the Climactic Struggle of History

Introduction

The Bible speaks with sobriety about a period of profound trial that accompanies the closing of this age. Scripture presents this season as one in which human rebellion reaches its full expression and God's purposes move toward decisive fulfillment. Christian theology has traditionally referred to this period as *the tribulation*. The doctrine does not arise from a single passage but from the convergence of prophetic, apocalyptic, and teaching texts that describe intense suffering, divine judgment, and the final opposition to God's reign (Jer. 30:7; Dan. 12:1; Matt. 24:21).[145]

This chapter examines the tribulation and the climactic struggle of history with careful attention to Scripture and with appropriate theological restraint. The aim is to explain the major interpretive approaches, clarify key biblical terms, and situate the doctrine within the larger story of God's redemptive purposes, without pressing speculative conclusions beyond what Scripture affirms.[146]

Defining the Tribulation

In biblical theology, the tribulation refers to a period of intensified distress associated with the culmination of history and the return of Jesus Christ. Several biblical texts describe this season as a time of unparalleled trouble, divine judgment, and testing for the world:

> Alas! That day is so great there is none like it;
> it is a time of distress for Jacob;
> yet he shall be saved out of it. (Jer. 30:7)

> And there shall be a time of trouble, such as never has been since there was a nation till that time. (Dan. 12:1)

> For then there will be great tribulation, such as has not been from the beginning of the world until now, no, and never will be. (Matt. 24:21)

The language of *tribulation* draws from prophetic imagery that portrays both judgment upon evil and purification for God's people.

Some theological traditions describe the tribulation as a future seven-year period, often connected to Daniel's prophecy of the seventy weeks (Dan. 9:24-27) and understood as the final "week" of that prophecy. Others understand the tribulation more broadly as the suffering that characterizes the entire church age, intensifying toward the end.[147] These differences arise from how interpreters relate prophetic symbolism, historical fulfillment, and apocalyptic imagery.

Biblical Background and Key Themes

The Old Testament frequently speaks of a coming "day of the Lord," a time when God acts decisively to judge wickedness and restore righteousness (Amos 5:18-20; Zeph. 1:14-18). These texts portray the day as both fearful and redemptive, emphasizing God's sovereignty over history and His commitment to justice.

The book of Daniel contributes significantly to later discussions of tribulation. Daniel's visions describe periods of oppression, blasphemous rulers, and severe persecution, followed by divine intervention and deliverance (Dan. 7-12). Daniel 9:24-27, in particular, introduces the concept of a final "week" associated with covenant fulfillment, judgment, and restoration. Interpretations of this passage shape many later views of the tribulation, especially within premillennial and dispensational traditions.[148]

In the New Testament, Jesus speaks of "great tribulation" in His Olivet Discourse, describing distress, deception, and persecution preceding His return (Matt. 24; Mark 13; Luke 21). He warns of false christs, wars, famines, earthquakes, and persecution of His followers, but also promises that "the one who endures to the end will be saved" (Matt. 24:13).

Paul echoes these themes by referring to rebellion, the revelation of a "man of lawlessness," and a climactic confrontation between truth and deception (2 Thess. 2:3-12). The book of Revelation presents a symbolic portrayal of judgment, conflict, and endurance through its cycles of seals, trumpets, and bowls (Rev. 6-16). While interpreters differ on whether these events are mostly past, present, or future, they agree that Revelation depicts both severe opposition to God's people and God's ultimate triumph.[149]

Major Interpretive Approaches

Christians have developed several interpretive frameworks to understand the tribulation. These approaches reflect differing ways of reading prophecy, relating Israel and the church, and interpreting apocalyptic symbolism.

Pretribulationism

Pretribulationism understands the tribulation as a future, seven-year period of global distress that follows the removal of the church through a pretribulational rapture and precedes Christ's millennial reign.[150] This view draws heavily from Daniel 9, 1 Thessalonians 4-5, and Revelation 6-18, as well as passages that speak of believers being kept from or delivered from coming wrath (1 Thess. 1:10; 5:9; Rev. 3:10).

Within this framework, the tribulation unfolds in two halves. The first half involves political realignment, covenant agreements, and increasing turmoil. The second half, often called "the great tribulation," features intensified persecution, the cessation of temple worship, and the open self-exaltation of a final adversary commonly associated with the "man of lawlessness" or "antichrist." Throughout this period, God's judgments unfold through symbolic sequences of seals, trumpets, and bowls, revealing both judgment and calls to repentance (Rev. 6-16).

This approach emphasizes God's sovereign control over history and His distinct purposes for Israel and the nations, culminating in Christ's victorious return and the establishment of His reign.

Historic and Post-tribulational Premillennialism

Other premillennial interpreters affirm a future tribulation but expect the church to endure it rather than be removed beforehand. Sometimes called *historic premillennialism* or *post-tribulational premillennialism*, this view holds that believers experience persecution and suffering during the end-time crisis yet remain under God's spiritual protection.[151]

The gathering of believers to Christ occurs at the time of His visible return, following this period of distress (Matt. 24:29-31; 1 Thess. 4:16-17). This approach emphasizes continuity between the church's present sufferings and the intensified trials of the last days, highlighting Jesus' calls to watchfulness and endurance.

Preterism

The term *preterism* comes from the Latin word *praeter*, meaning "past" or "that which has gone before." As an interpretive approach, preterism holds that many biblical prophecies—especially those related to tribulation, judgment, and cosmic upheaval—refer primarily to events that occurred in the past rather than to a still-future global crisis.

Preterist interpretations understand many tribulation-related prophecies as having been fulfilled in the first century, particularly in the events surrounding the destruction of Jerusalem in AD 70. According to this approach, Jesus' warnings in Matthew 24 and significant portions of the book of Revelation describe God's historical judgment on Jerusalem and the Roman world, using vivid apocalyptic imagery common to Jewish prophetic literature.

Most preterists affirm a future return of Christ, the resurrection of the dead, and a final judgment, while viewing tribulation language as symbolically portraying first-century events with enduring theological significance. This perspective often aligns with amillennial or postmillennial interpretations of Revelation 20.[152]

Broader Church-Age Tribulation Approaches

Many amillennial and postmillennial interpreters understand tribulation more broadly as the suffering and opposition experienced by God's people throughout the entire church age, culminating in an intensified struggle before Christ's return (Acts 14:22; Rev. 1:9).[153] In this view, the "great tribulation" is not confined strictly to a seven-year period but represents the gathered force of persecution and evil that will reach its peak just prior to the final victory of Christ.

The Climactic Struggle of History

Across these interpretive approaches, Scripture consistently portrays a final confrontation in which human rebellion, spiritual deception, and opposition to God's reign reach their fullest expression before being decisively overcome by Christ. This struggle does not emerge suddenly but represents the culmination of patterns already present throughout redemptive history.

Biblical teaching frequently describes this conflict in personal and symbolic terms. The New Testament speaks of figures such as the "man of lawlessness" (2 Thess. 2:3-12) and "antichrist" (1 John 2:18; 4:3), not primarily to satisfy curiosity, but to alert the church to the concentrated form that rebellion against God may assume near the end. These figures embody resistance to divine authority, self-exaltation, and deception, drawing together political, religious, and spiritual opposition to Christ.[154]

The book of Revelation depicts this climactic struggle through vivid apocalyptic imagery. The dragon, the beasts, and the false prophet represent coordinated forces of evil that seek to oppose God's purposes and persecute His people (Rev. 12-13). At the same time, Revelation emphasizes the perseverance of the saints, who remain faithful through suffering and bear witness to Christ even in the face of death:[155]

> And they have conquered him by the blood of the Lamb and by the word of their testimony, for they loved not their lives even unto death. (Rev. 12:11)

Throughout Scripture, this final struggle is framed by divine sovereignty. God permits evil to reach its appointed limit, while directing history toward its resolution. The gathering of hostile powers, the intensification of deception, and the persecution of God's people all move toward a single outcome: the appearing of Jesus Christ, who defeats His enemies and establishes His reign (Rev. 19:11-21; 1 Cor. 15:24-28).

Points of Theological Agreement

Despite differing interpretations of the tribulation's timing and scope, Christians broadly affirm several foundational truths:

- God sovereignly governs history and its conclusion.
- Evil and suffering do not escape God's authority or final judgment.
- Christ will return in power and glory to bring history to its appointed end.
- Faithful endurance and holiness characterize the calling of God's people in every age (Matt. 24:13; Rev. 14:12).

These shared convictions provide a stable theological center amid interpretive diversity and help keep the focus on what Scripture clearly emphasizes.

Pastoral Reflection

The doctrine of the tribulation directs the church to confidence in God's faithfulness amid trial. Scripture presents hardship as neither meaningless nor ultimate. Jesus tells His disciples, "In the world you will have tribulation. But take heart; I have overcome the world" (John 16:33).

For believers, the tribulation theme reinforces perseverance, hope, and trust.[156] It directs attention toward Christ's promised return and the certainty that evil will not endure. The climactic struggle of history culminates in redemption, restoration, and the reign of Christ. Until that day, the church walks forward in faith, resolved in the promise that nothing "will be able to separate us from the love of God in Christ Jesus our Lord" (Rom. 8:39).

Conclusion

The doctrine of the tribulation brings together themes of judgment, endurance, and hope. Scripture portrays a period of profound struggle that moves history toward its resolution under Christ's lordship. While interpretations differ in detail, the biblical witness affirms God's sovereignty, the certainty of Christ's victory, and the calling of the church to faithful endurance. A conservative evangelical approach seeks to affirm what Scripture clearly teaches, to acknowledge areas of legitimate difference, and to let the promise of Christ's triumph sustain the people of God in every generation.[157]

Part Five

Judgment

Chapter 13

The Final Judgment Before God

Introduction

Christian Scripture consistently affirms that history is moving toward a divinely appointed conclusion. The doctrine of the Final Judgment proclaims that when Jesus Christ returns in glory, every human life will be brought into the light of God's perfect righteousness. This event stands at the center of Christian hope and accountability.[158] It assures believers that evil will not endure forever, that justice will be rendered without error, and that God's redemptive purposes will reach their completion.

The Final Judgment does not portray God as uncertain or reactive. Scripture presents this moment as the outworking of God's eternal plan, entrusted to the risen Son.[159] As Jesus Himself declares, "The Father judges no one, but has given all judgment to the Son" (John 5:22). The One who gave His life for the world will also stand as its Judge.

Defining the Final Judgment

The doctrine of the Final Judgment teaches that all people—living and dead—will be raised and brought before Jesus Christ to give an account of their lives. Jesus says,

> An hour is coming when all who are in the tombs will hear his voice and come out, those who have done good to the resurrection of life, and those who have done evil to the resurrection of judgment. (John 5:28-29)

This judgment reveals God's perfect justice and His perfect mercy. Scripture affirms that each person will receive an eternal destiny: eternal life in the presence of God or eternal separation from Him (Matt. 25:46; John 5:28-29; 2 Thess. 1:8-9).[160]

The Final Judgment confirms that human history is purposeful. Life unfolds under God's moral governance, and every act, word, and allegiance ultimately matter (Eccl. 12:14; Rom. 2:5-11). God's judgment restores what sin has distorted, exposes what has been hidden, and brings creation into righteous order.[161]

Christ the Judge of All

The New Testament consistently places the Final Judgment in the hands of Jesus Christ, highlighting both His divine authority and His redemptive mission.[162] Judgment is not entrusted to an abstract principle or impersonal force but to the risen Son who fully shares in God's holiness, justice, and mercy. Jesus Himself declares, "The Father judges no one, but has given all judgment to the Son" (John 5:22). This assignment of judgment underscores Christ's unique role as mediator between God and humanity.

Scripture emphasizes that the One who judges the world is the same One who entered the world in humility, bore human suffering, and offered Himself for sinners. Jesus speaks of His return as the Son of Man who come in glory, seated on His throne, to gather all nations before Him (Matt. 25:31-32). This scene unites kingship and judgment, showing that Christ's authority over history reaches its full expression at the end of the age.

Paul reinforces this Christ-centered vision by teaching that God "has fixed a day on which he will judge the world in righteousness by a man whom he has appointed," giving assurance to all by raising Him from the dead (Acts 17:31). The resurrection publicly confirms Jesus as both Lord and Judge. Final Judgment, therefore, flows directly from Christ's victory over sin and death. As 1 Corinthians 15:20-28 explains, the risen Christ reigns until every enemy is placed under His feet, and death itself is destroyed.[163]

John's vision in Revelation 20:11-15 further centers judgment on Christ's authority. All the dead stand before God as the books are opened, revealing the truth of every life. The presence of the Book of Life highlights that judgment is inseparably connected to redemption: those who belong to Christ stand secure, not because of their perfection, but because of His saving work.[164]

By presenting Christ as Judge, Scripture teaches that Final Judgment is neither arbitrary nor detached from grace. The Judge is the Lamb who was slain (Rev. 5:6).[165] His wounds testify that judgment has already been borne for those who trust in Him. Justice and mercy, holiness and grace, meet in the person Jesus Christ.

Judgment According to Works and Salvation by Grace

Scripture repeatedly affirms that judgment takes human works seriously. Jesus describes a final separation between the righteous and the unrighteous, using the imagery of sheep and goats (Matt. 25:31-46). The righteous demonstrate lives marked by mercy, compassion, and faithfulness, while the unrighteous reveal hearts resistant to God's reign.

When Scripture is read as a unified witness, a clear theological pattern emerges: salvation comes by grace through faith, and genuine faith expresses itself through transformed living (Eph. 2:8-10). Works do not earn salvation; they testify to the reality of faith. As James writes, "So also faith by itself, if it does not have works, is dead" (James 2:17).

Jesus illustrates this gracious economy in the Parable of the Workers in the Vineyard (Matt. 20:1-16). Each worker receives the same reward, grounded in the generosity of the master rather than the length of service.

At the Final Judgment, God's verdict reveals the authenticity of faith by the fruit it has produced, while remaining entirely grounded in Christ's saving work. In this way, the Bible can speak both of judgment "according to what they had done" (Rev. 20:13) and of salvation "not a result of works, so that no one may boast" (Eph. 2:9). Judgment according to works discloses what a person has truly trusted and loved; it does not replace the cross as the ground of acceptance with God. For the believer, good works are the evidence of union with Christ, not the price of entry into His kingdom.[166]

Judgment of Believers: Reward and Accountability

Scripture teaches that believers in Christ will stand before Him for an evaluation of their lives, not to determine their salvation, but to assess their faithfulness. This judgment is often called the *judgment seat of Christ* (cf. Rom. 14:10-12; 2 Cor. 5:10). It focuses on how believers have lived in response to the grace they have already received.

Paul explains that Christ Himself is the only foundation upon which a believer's life can be built: "For no one can lay a foundation other than that which is laid, which is Jesus Christ" (1 Cor. 3:11). Every Christian builds on that foundation through choices, actions, obedience, and service. At the Final Judgment, these works are tested—not to re-expose sin already forgiven, but to reveal their true spiritual value. Works shaped by faith, love, and obedience endure and receive reward; works driven by pride, self-interest, or misplaced priorities do not endure (1 Cor. 3:12-14).

Importantly, this judgment never places a believer's salvation in question.[167] Paul is explicit: even if a believer's works are largely burned away, "he himself will be saved, but only as through fire" (1 Cor. 3:15). Salvation rests entirely on Christ's finished work, not on the believer's performance. Judgment for believers, therefore, is an expression of God's fatherly care, not His condemning wrath (Rom. 8:1).

Scripture consistently presents this judgment as an occasion of affirmation and reward. Jesus speaks of faithful servants entering into the joy of their Master and being entrusted with greater responsibility (Matt. 25:21; Luke 19:17). The New Testament describes rewards such as crowns (2 Tim. 4:8; James 1:12; 1 Pet. 5:4) and praise from God (1 Cor. 4:5), all of which ultimately glorify Christ rather than human achievement.[168]

For believers, then, the Final Judgment is not a moment of fear, but of accountability shaped by grace. It confirms that faithfulness matters, that obedience is seen, and that no labor done for Christ is wasted (1 Cor. 15:58).

Judgment of Unbelievers

Scripture speaks with clarity and sobriety about the judgment faced by those who persist in unbelief. Unlike the judgment of believers, which evaluates faithfulness within a secure relationship to Christ, the judgment of unbelievers addresses accountability for sin apart from saving faith. This judgment concerns one's standing before God and results in eternal separation from Him.

Jesus consistently warned that rejection of God's truth carries eternal consequences. In Matthew 7:22-23, He describes individuals who appeal to religious activity and outward works, yet remain unknown to Him. Their judgment reveals that proximity to religious practice cannot substitute for repentance, faith, and obedience. Relationship with Christ, not external association, determines one's eternal destiny.

The clearest depiction of this judgment appears in Revelation 20:11-15. John sees all the dead standing before God as the books are opened, representing the full record of human life. Those whose names are not found written in the Book of Life are judged according to their deeds and thrown into the lake of fire. This judgment reflects God's perfect justice: every life is assessed truthfully, without partiality or error.

Scripture emphasizes that this judgment is neither arbitrary nor cruel. God's wrath is portrayed as righteous response to persistent rebellion and rejection of grace. Paul describes the outcome as being "away from the presence of the Lord and from the glory of his might" (2 Thess. 1:9). This separation represents the tragic, self-chosen outcome of loving darkness rather than the light (John 3:19-20).[169]

Unlike believers, unbelievers face judgment without the covering of Christ's atoning work. The gospel consistently teaches that Christ alone bore judgment for sin, and those who reject Him remain accountable for their own guilt (John 3:18). This distinction underscores the seriousness of the Final Judgment and the urgency of the gospel message. Yet even here, Scripture maintains God's moral integrity: He is "not wishing that any should perish, but that all should reach repentance" (2 Pet. 3:9). For this reason, Christians speak of the Final Judgment with both gravity and tears. Scripture permits no delight in the perishing of the wicked (Ezek. 33:11), but it does call believers to rest in the wisdom and goodness of God, who knows every heart perfectly. The proper response is not speculation about who will be saved without Christ, but renewed urgency to make Christ known and renewed trust that the Judge of all the earth will do what is right.[170]

Judgment of Angels and the Defeat of Evil

The biblical vision of Final Judgment extends beyond humanity. Paul indicates that redeemed believers "will judge angels" (1 Cor. 6:3), suggesting that the people of God will share in Christ's verdict over rebellious spiritual powers.

Revelation 19-20 depicts the binding and final judgment of Satan and the destruction of death itself.

The devil is cast into the lake of fire (Rev. 20:10), and death and Hades are likewise destroyed (Rev. 20:14). Evil reaches its end, and God's kingdom stands uncontested. This judgment brings restoration as well as justice, bringing creation into a state free from corruption, violence, and fear.[171]

The Final Judgment and the Renewal of Creation

The Final Judgment prepares the way for the full renewal of creation. Scripture presents judgment as the decisive act through which God removes corruption and establishes righteousness in the world. Judgment brings history to its rightful resolution by addressing sin, defeating evil, and restoring creation to its intended order under Christ's reign.

Peter teaches that the present heavens and earth are "stored up for fire" (2 Pet. 3:7), not for annihilation, but for transformation. He declares that God's people look forward to "new heavens and a new earth in which righteousness dwells" (2 Pet. 3:13). Judgment functions as purification: what is opposed to God's holiness is exposed and removed so that creation can be renewed rather than abandoned.

This is the theme seen in the broader biblical story. The curse introduced through human rebellion brought decay, violence, and death into the world (Gen. 3; Rom. 8:20-22). Final Judgment marks the decisive reversal of that curse.[172] Paul explains that creation itself longs for liberation and will share in "the freedom of the children of God" (Rom. 8:21). When Christ judges the world, He completes this work of liberation by bringing creation into harmony with God's righteous will.

Revelation presents this renewal vividly. Following the Final Judgment, John sees a new heaven and a new earth, where death, mourning, and pain no longer exist (Rev. 21:1-4). The removal of evil through judgment allows God's dwelling presence to fill creation without obstruction. Justice clears the way for peace, and judgment opens the door to lasting restoration.

The Final Judgment, therefore, stands as a hopeful doctrine. God does not judge in order to destroy His world, but to heal it.

Judgment fulfills God's covenant purposes by bringing creation to its intended goal: a renewed world fully ordered by righteousness, life, and the presence of God with His people.

Living in Light of the Final Judgment

The doctrine of the Final Judgment shapes Christian life in the present. Scripture calls believers to live with holiness, mercy, and perseverance because Christ will return as Judge (1 Thess. 5:1-10; 2 Pet. 3:11-14). Awareness of judgment nurtures vigilance, compassion, and integrity.[173]

Believers live as children of the light, guided by hope rather than fear. The certainty of Christ's return gives urgency to mission, seriousness to repentance, and courage in suffering. Knowing that every hidden thing will be brought to light (Eccl. 12:14; 1 Cor. 4:5) encourages faithful obedience even when recognition is absent, and injustice appears to prevail.

Pastoral Conclusion

For those who belong to Christ, the Final Judgment marks not the collapse of hope but its fulfillment. Every injustice meets God's righteousness. Every hidden sorrow receives His compassion. Every faithful act finds its place in God's remembrance and reward.

The Judge of all the earth is also the Savior who bore judgment in our place. Believers stand before Him clothed in grace, not condemnation. This promise steadies the heart and directs the life of faith. Christians live today with confidence, purpose, and hope, trusting the One who will judge the world in righteousness and welcome His people into the joy of His presence. The doctrine of the Final Judgment, rightly received, does not drive the church to fear but to worship, repentance, and steadfast obedience as it awaits the day when God will be "all in all" (1 Cor. 15:28).[174]

Part Six

The Eternal State

Chapter 14

The Eternal Blessedness of the Righteous

Introduction

This chapter aims to guide the reader toward a clear, biblically grounded understanding of the believer's eternal hope. It gathers the promises of resurrection, judgment, and renewal to show how Scripture presents the final destiny of the righteous as the fullness of life with God—secure, joyful, and everlasting.[175]

Eternal blessedness refers to the final and everlasting condition of those who belong to Christ, in which they enjoy unbroken life with God—fully restored in body and soul, free from sin and death, and filled with enduring joy in His presence.[176] Throughout the doctrine of last things, Scripture consistently directs the believer's gaze forward. The return of Christ, the resurrection of the dead, and the final judgment stand together, pointing toward a single goal: the full and eternal blessedness of God's redeemed people.[177] This chapter gathers that hope into focus.

The Bible presents the future of the righteous in terms of resurrection, transformation, communion, and joy secured by

God's promise. The final state of the righteous describes life as God intended it from the beginning—renewed, glorified, and forever secure in His presence.

The Resurrection of the Righteous

Scripture teaches with clarity that God will raise the dead, and this resurrection stands at the center of Christian hope. Daniel foretells a future awakening of those who sleep in the dust, leading to everlasting life:

> And many of those who sleep in the dust of the earth shall awake, some to everlasting life, and some to shame and everlasting contempt. (Dan. 12:2)

Jesus confirmed this promise and placed Himself at its center, declaring that all who are in the graves will hear His voice and rise:

> Do not marvel at this, for an hour is coming when all who are in the tombs will hear his voice and come out, those who have done good to the resurrection of life, and those who have done evil to the resurrection of judgment. (John 5:28-29)

The New Testament repeatedly affirms this future resurrection. Paul proclaims before Felix that he has "a hope in God...that there will be a resurrection of both the just and the unjust" (Acts 24:15). The resurrection of the righteous rests securely on the resurrection of Christ Himself. In 1 Corinthians 15, Paul explains that Christ's resurrection is "the firstfruits of those who have fallen asleep," guaranteeing that those who belong to Him will be raised (1 Cor. 15:20–23).[178]

For the righteous, resurrection brings God's people into new life, free from decay and death. Resurrection marks the definitive victory of Christ over the grave and confirms the believer's eternal future.[179]

Judgment and Vindication for the Righteous

Following the resurrection, Scripture teaches that all people will appear before Christ. For believers, this judgment evaluates faithfulness but not whether they belong to Him. Christ has already borne condemnation (Rom. 8:1). This moment reveals faithfulness, obedience, and service rendered in response to grace.

Paul describes this evaluation as the judgment seat of Christ:

> For we will all stand before the judgment seat of God. (Rom. 14:10)

> For we must all appear before the judgment seat of Christ, so that each one may receive what is due for what he has done in the body, whether good or evil. (2 Cor. 5:10)

Christ examines the believer's life to disclose its true spiritual value. Faithful works receive reward; works lacking eternal substance pass away. Salvation remains secure, grounded in Christ alone (1 Cor. 3:11-15).[180]

This judgment vindicates God's people publicly. Christ acknowledges their faith, honors their perseverance, and confirms that no labor done in His name was wasted (Matt. 25:21; 1 Cor. 15:58). For the righteous, judgment becomes a moment of joy and affirmation, not fear.[181]

Eternal Life in the Presence of God

After the resurrection and judgment, the righteous enter their eternal state. Scripture consistently describes this future as life with God Himself. Eternal life means unbroken communion with the Creator, sustained joy, and complete restoration.[182]

Revelation describes this reality with striking clarity:

> Behold, the dwelling place of God is with man. He will dwell with them, and they will be his people, and God himself will be with them as their God. He will wipe away every tear from their eyes, and death shall be no more, neither shall there be mourning, nor crying, nor pain anymore, for the former things have passed away. (Rev. 21:3-4)

In this future, God removes every trace of sorrow, pain, and death. Life unfolds in righteousness, peace, and joy under His immediate presence. Eternal blessedness centers on relationship with God: the redeemed live in direct fellowship with God within a perfected environment. Scripture teaches that "in your presence there is fullness of joy; at your right hand are pleasures forevermore" (Ps. 16:11).

The Beatific Vision: Seeing God

At the heart of eternal blessedness stands the beatific vision—the direct and unhindered sight of God. Scripture presents this hope as the deepest fulfillment of human longing, while also testifying to humanity's longstanding inability to endure such a vision in a fallen state.

From the earliest pages of Scripture, humanity's relationship with God is marked by distance. After the Fall, Adam and Eve are driven from the garden, away from the immediate presence of God (Gen. 3:22-24). The desire for restored communion remains, but access to God's unveiled presence becomes dangerous for sinful humanity. When Moses asks to see God's glory, the Lord responds that no one can see His face and live

(Exod. 33:18-20). Moses receives a partial revelation, hidden in the cleft of the rock, signaling both God's nearness and the limits imposed by human sinfulness.

This pattern continues throughout the Old Testament. Israel encounters God through mediated signs—fire, cloud, temple, sacrifice—yet never through direct sight. Isaiah's vision of the Lord in the temple leads immediately to a confession of unworthiness and fear (Isa. 6:1-5). The psalmist gives voice to a longing that remains unfulfilled in this life: "As for me, I shall behold your face in righteousness" (Ps. 17:15). Job expresses the same hope in the midst of suffering, declaring confidence that he will one day see God with his own eyes (Job 19:25-27).

The New Testament reveals that this longing finds its fulfillment in Christ.[183] Jesus declares that the pure in heart will see God (Matt. 5:8), locating the promise of vision within the work of redemption. Through Christ, believers begin to behold God by faith. Paul explains that even now believers "beholding the glory of the Lord, are being transformed into the same image from one degree of glory to another" (2 Cor. 3:18). Yet this present vision remains real but incomplete.

Paul describes the present condition as partial sight that awaits completion: "Now we see in a mirror dimly, but then face to face" (1 Cor. 13:12). John echoes this hope: "We know that when he appears we shall be like him, because we shall see him as he is" (1 John 3:2).[184] The barrier introduced by sin finally falls away; sight and transformation coincide.

Revelation brings this promise to its climactic fulfillment:

> They will see his face, and his name will be on their foreheads. (Rev. 22:4)

In the renewed creation, the redeemed no longer encounter God through shadow or symbol. The vision that once brought fear now brings joy. The sight once fatal to fallen humanity becomes the source of eternal life and delight. Seeing God completes redemption, satisfies the deepest human longing, and fulfills the purpose for which humanity was created.[185]

The Glorified Body

Eternal blessedness includes the redemption of the body. Scripture affirms that God renews both the physical world and the human body. The resurrection body remains truly physical while fully transformed, designed for life in the unveiled presence of God.

From the beginning, Scripture presents the human body as an essential part of God's good creation (Gen. 1:26-31). Salvation in Christ does not abandon embodiment but restores it. Paul insists that resurrection involves both continuity and transformation:

> What is sown is perishable; what is raised is imperishable. It is sown in dishonor; it is raised in glory. It is sown in weakness; it is raised in power. It is sown a natural body; it is raised a spiritual body. (1 Cor. 15:42-44)

Resurrection does not replace the body; it redeems it.

The risen body of Jesus provides the definitive pattern for the glorified body. After His resurrection, Jesus could be seen, touched, and recognized by His disciples. He ate with them and spoke with them, confirming the physical reality of His resurrection (Luke 24:39-43; John 20:27). At the same time, His body displayed new qualities consistent with resurrection life.[186] He appeared suddenly among His disciples and lived beyond the reach of suffering and death (Rom. 6:9).

Paul describes the glorified body using a series of contrasts that emphasize transformation: perishable raised imperishable, dishonor raised in glory, weakness raised in power (1 Cor. 15:42-43). He calls it a "spiritual body," meaning one animated and governed by the Spirit rather than limited by sin and decay. This body remains personal, recognizable, and embodied, yet free from corruption.

Scripture gives further insight into what believers may expect. The glorified body knows no sickness, disability, or death. Revelation describes renewed creation where mourning, pain, and death no longer exist (Rev. 21:4). The body no longer resists obedience or worship but serves God with perfect harmony between desire and action.[187]

Paul assures believers that Christ "will transform our lowly body to be like his glorious body" (Phil. 3:20-21). This transformation prepares believers for eternal joy, worship, and service. God fits His people completely for life in His presence, ensuring that nothing within them limits their capacity to delight in Him forever.

Life in the Renewed Creation

The eternal blessedness of the righteous unfolds within the new heavens and the new earth. Scripture portrays this future as a renewed creation in which God restores the world to its intended harmony under Christ's reign.[188]

The prophets anticipated this restored world in concrete and hopeful terms. Isaiah describes a renewed creation marked by peace, justice, and flourishing life, where violence and disorder no longer define human existence (Isa. 11:6-9; 65:17-25). These images communicate stability, abundance, and security under God's righteous rule. Creation itself reflects God's peace as His will is fully realized.

The New Testament deepens this vision. Paul teaches that creation, which now groans under the weight of corruption, will share in the freedom and glory of the children of God (Rom. 8:19-21). Renewal reaches beyond individual salvation to encompass the entire created order; God liberates creation from decay and establishes it in righteousness.

Revelation 21—22 offers the most complete biblical picture of life in the renewed creation. God dwells openly with His people, filling the world with His presence. Light flows from God Himself, removing all darkness (Rev. 21:23). Life flourishes around the throne of God, symbolized by the river of life and the tree whose leaves bring healing to the nations (Rev. 22:1-2). The curse no longer shapes human experience (Rev. 22:3).[189]

Life in the renewed creation includes meaningful activity. Scripture speaks of the redeemed reigning with Christ, serving Him, and participating fully in the life of His kingdom (Rev. 22:5; 2 Tim. 2:12). Worship and work unite seamlessly as every action reflects devotion to God.[190] Relationships unfold without sin, fear, or division.

Eternal life remains dynamic and rich. Scripture presents the future as unending growth in joy, wisdom, and knowledge of God. The redeemed continue to delight in God's goodness and explore the richness of His creation forever. Life in the renewed creation expresses fullness, purpose, and joy in the presence of the Lord.

Conclusion

The doctrine of eternal blessedness gathers every promise of resurrection, judgment, and renewal into a single horizon of hope.[191] Scripture presents the believer's future as a certain destiny secured by the finished work of Christ: God raises His people, restores their bodies, renews creation, and brings them into enduring life in His presence.

This future shapes the present life of faith. The promise of eternal blessedness grounds perseverance, strengthens obedience, and gives lasting meaning to service and sacrifice. Because the future stands secure in Christ, believers labor with confidence, trusting that every act of faithfulness carries eternal significance (1 Cor. 15:58).[192]

Eternal blessedness also orients the believer's heart and hope. Life unfolds with confidence and expectation, guided by the certainty that God completes what He has begun (Phil 1:6). Resurrection, communion with God, glory, and unending life await all who belong to Christ. This hope steadies the heart, strengthens faith, and directs discipleship toward its appointed end.

The risen and reigning Savior will finish His work. He will raise His people, dwell with them forever, and fill their lives with joy in His presence. Eternal blessedness stands as the fulfillment of God's purpose for humanity and creation—life restored, renewed, and fully enjoyed in fellowship with Him forever.

Chapter 15

The Judgment of the Wicked

Introduction: The Necessity of Final Justice

This chapter addresses one of the most sobering doctrines in Christian theology: the judgment of the wicked. Scripture presents this teaching with clarity and seriousness because it arises directly from the character of God. The God who saves is also the God who judges. His judgment flows from His holiness, righteousness, and unwavering commitment to truth. The final judgment does not stand in tension with divine love; it reveals the moral seriousness of a world created to reflect God's goodness.[193]

The judgment of the wicked refers to God's final, righteous, and everlasting verdict upon those who persist in unbelief and refuse repentance. This judgment confirms that evil does not endure forever, injustice does not go unanswered, and rebellion against God carries real and eternal consequences. Scripture presents this doctrine not to satisfy curiosity or provoke fear, but to uphold God's justice and magnify the grace offered in Christ (Rom. 2:5-8; John 3:16-18).[194]

God's Righteous Character and the Necessity of Judgment

Scripture consistently teaches that God acts in perfect righteousness. He calls His image-bearers to reflect His holiness and holds them accountable for their response to His revelation. God's justice requires that He judge evil; He does not ignore sin or treat wickedness as inconsequential.[195] Judgment flows from who God is.

The Old and New Testaments affirm this truth repeatedly. Ecclesiastes declares that "God will bring every deed into judgment, with every secret thing, whether good or evil" (Eccl. 12:14). Jesus warns that human beings "will give account on the day of judgment for every careless word they speak" (Matt. 12:36). The book of Revelation portrays God responding decisively to injustice and oppression with righteous judgment as the martyrs cry, "O Sovereign Lord, holy and true, how long before you will judge and avenge our blood?" (Rev. 6:10; cf. Rev. 16:5–7; 19:1–2).

Paul proclaims this certainty in Athens, declaring that God "has fixed a day on which he will judge the world in righteousness by a man whom he has appointed," giving assurance of this by raising Him from the dead (Acts 17:31). Human conscience itself confirms this truth. Romans teaches that people "know God's decree that those who practice such things deserve to die" (Rom. 1:32), even when they suppress that knowledge. God's judgment arises from His holiness and reflects His faithfulness to truth.[196]

Biblical Language for Divine Judgment

Scripture uses weighty language to describe God's judgment of the wicked. Terms such as *wrath, punishment, condemnation, destruction,* and *vengeance* appear throughout the biblical witness. These terms do not describe uncontrolled anger or cruelty. They communicate measured, purposeful, and righteous action.[197]

Paul repeatedly speaks of "the righteous judgment of God" (Rom. 2:5; 2 Thess. 1:5). God's judgment reflects moral precision. He judges with perfect knowledge, free from error and excess. His wrath is His holy opposition to sin, not a loss of self-control (Rom. 1:18). Judgment stands as an expression of God's commitment to justice rather than a departure from His goodness.

Proportionate Justice in the Final Judgment

Scripture teaches that God judges according to truth, proportion, and moral reality. Proportionate justice means that God's judgment responds fittingly to human action and responsibility. It reflects neither impulse nor excess but careful moral assessment rooted in God's perfect knowledge.

Romans 2:5-16 explains that God "will render to each one according to his works" (Rom. 2:6), not as a system of earning salvation, but as the disclosure of each person's response to God's revelation.[198] Deeds reveal allegiance, priorities, and the posture of the heart toward God. Those who persist in unbelief demonstrate their rejection of truth through consistent patterns of action (Rom. 2:8-9).

Jesus teaches clearly that accountability corresponds to knowledge and opportunity. He declares that cities which witnessed His miracles yet refused repentance will face greater judgment than those who received less revelation (Matt. 11:20-24). He explains that servants entrusted with greater responsibility answer for greater neglect, while those with limited knowledge face proportionate accountability (Luke 12:47-48). These teachings establish that divine judgment accounts for degree, not merely category.[199]

Revelation reinforces this principle by depicting books opened before God's throne, recording every deed with exactness:

> And the dead were judged by what was written in the books, according to what they had done. (Rev. 20:12)

Judgment proceeds from complete truth rather than general accusation. Nothing is overlooked, exaggerated, or forgotten. God renders judgment with precision that matches reality.

Retributive justice therefore affirms that God's judgment remains personal, fair, and measured. Each individual stands accountable for their response to truth, and judgment reflects the full moral weight of a life lived either toward or away from God. Divine justice does not operate with arbitrariness; it displays the integrity of God's holiness.

The Final Judgment and the Day of the Lord

Scripture identifies the final judgment with the return of Christ. The prophets refer to this event as "the Day of the Lord," a decisive moment when God acts publicly to judge evil and establish righteousness (Isa. 2:12; Amos 5:18-20; Zeph. 1:14-18). The New Testament applies this expectation directly to Jesus Christ.

Revelation 20:11-15 presents the Great White Throne judgment, the final judicial scene of human history. John describes a cosmic courtroom where heaven and earth flee before the holy presence of God, underscoring the absolute authority and purity of the Judge:

> Then I saw a great white throne and him who was seated on it. From his presence earth and sky fled away, and no place was found for them. (Rev. 20:11)

All the dead are raised and stand before the throne, and books are opened that record every life with complete accuracy. Another book—the Book of Life—reveals who belongs to Christ (Rev. 20:12). This judgment is universal, public, and decisive, bringing God's moral order to its final and unchallenged conclusion. Those whose names do not appear in the Book of Life are "thrown into the lake of fire" (Rev. 20:15).[200] Christ stands as Judge, executing justice with authority given by the Father (John 5:22-29).

The Reality and Nature of Hell

Scripture presents hell as the final outcome of divine judgment upon the wicked. Hell represents conscious, ongoing separation from the gracious presence of God, under His righteous wrath. Biblical imagery communicates the seriousness of this condition through descriptions of fire, darkness, exclusion, and destruction.

Jesus speaks of "the eternal fire prepared for the devil and his angels" and of the wicked going away "into eternal punishment, but the righteous into eternal life" (Matt. 25:41, 46). He warns of "hell [Gehenna], where their worm does not die and the fire is not quenched" (Mark 9:48). Revelation portrays the devil, the beast, and the false prophet thrown into the lake of fire, where "they will be tormented day and night forever and ever" (Rev. 20:10).

From a conservative evangelical perspective, these texts support the conclusion that hell is eternal (Matt. 25:46), just (Dan. 12:2), severe (Mark 9:43-48), and final (Rev. 20:14-15).[201] Jesus speaks of hell more frequently than any other figure in Scripture. His warnings express urgency and compassion; He calls sinners to repentance and faith, offering escape from judgment through Himself (Luke 13:3; John 3:16).

Hell results from persistent rejection of God's grace. Scripture never portrays hell as God's unwillingness to save, but as the rightful consequence of unrepentant unbelief and love of darkness rather than light (John 3:19-20).

The Nature of the Punishment of the Wicked

The nature of the punishment of the wicked refers to the character, basis, and moral purpose of God's final judgment upon those who die in persistent unbelief. Scripture presents this punishment as just, conscious, and irrevocable, arising not from divine cruelty but from God's holy response to unrepentant sin and sustained rejection of His grace.[202]

The Old Testament lays the foundation for understanding final judgment. The prophets speak of the Day of the Lord as a time of reckoning for covenant unfaithfulness (Amos 5:18-27). Judgment arises from persistent rebellion rather than momentary failure. Yet even within judgment, God preserves a redeemed remnant, pointing forward to new covenant renewal (Isa. 10:20-22; Jer. 31:31-34).

Daniel describes a resurrection leading either to everlasting life or everlasting contempt (Dan. 12:2). Isaiah portrays the fate of the wicked in terms of unending decay and fire: "their worm shall not die, their fire shall not be quenched" (Isa. 66:24). These images communicate finality and seriousness rather than speculative detail.[203]

Jesus places Himself at the center of this judgment. He identifies as the Son of Man who judges the nations (Dan. 7:13-14; Matt. 25:31-46). Through His teaching, Jesus exposes hearts and announces verdicts ahead of time through the call to repentance. Rejection of Christ reveals itself through persistent injustice, lack of mercy, and refusal to love others (Matt. 25:41-45).

Paul echoes this teaching by describing the fate of the wicked as "eternal destruction, away from the presence of the Lord and from the glory of his might" (2 Thess. 1:9). This outcome reflects the settled posture of a life resistant to grace.[204]

Revelation portrays final judgment symbolically yet decisively. Humanity receives repeated calls to repentance (Rev. 14:6-7; 16:9, 11), many refuse, and judgment follows. Those who oppose God's reign share the destiny of Satan and his allies in the lake of fire (Rev. 20:10, 14-15). Scripture presents this judgment as just, final, and irrevocable.

The Duration of the Punishment of the Wicked

Throughout Christian history, the duration of punishment has received sustained theological attention because it touches directly on God's justice, the seriousness of sin, and the finality of divine judgment. While Scripture speaks with clarity about the reality of judgment, believers have wrestled with how biblical language should be understood when describing its permanence.

The historic teaching of the church affirms that final judgment results in an enduring state of separation from God.

Roman Catholic, Protestant, and Eastern Orthodox traditions have consistently upheld this conviction, even while differing in emphasis and imagery. Across these traditions, the church has confessed that judgment is not temporary or symbolic, but lasting and consequential.

Alternative interpretations have arisen at various points in church history. Universal restoration proposes that all people will eventually be reconciled to God. Annihilationism argues that the wicked ultimately cease to exist rather than endure ongoing punishment. Other modern proposals attempt to reinterpret biblical language in less literal terms. Each of these views seeks to resolve the emotional and moral weight of the doctrine, yet each struggles to account for the full scope of Scripture's teaching.[205]

The New Testament repeatedly speaks of eternal punishment alongside eternal life, using parallel language that links duration in both destinies:

> And these will go away into eternal punishment, but the righteous into eternal life. (Matt. 25:46)

Daniel 12:2 likewise speaks of "everlasting life" and "shame and everlasting contempt" in the same breath. This symmetry forms a central pillar of the church's historic interpretation. From an evangelical and Southern Baptist perspective, the cumulative witness of Scripture affirms that the punishment of the wicked endures eternally, highlighting the gravity of sin, the holiness of God, and the immeasurable worth of Christ's saving work.[206]

Conclusion: Judgment, Mercy, and the Call to Repentance

The judgment of the wicked reveals the moral seriousness of God's world. Scripture teaches that history moves toward a just conclusion in which evil receives its due and righteousness prevails. God's judgment vindicates His holiness and confirms that injustice never holds the final word (Rev. 19:1-2).

This doctrine also magnifies grace. The same God who judges offers salvation through His Son. Christ stands as both Judge and Savior. The cross remains open testimony that God desires repentance and life rather than condemnation: "The Lord...is patient toward you, not wishing that any should perish, but that all should reach repentance" (2 Pet. 3:9; cf. John 3:16-17).

For believers, this doctrine deepens gratitude and strengthens compassion. For the church, it fuels urgency in evangelism and faithfulness in witness (Rom. 10:14-15; Jude 22-23). For all people, it stands as a sober summons to respond to God's grace while the door of mercy remains open.[207]

The Judge of all the earth rules with perfect justice and steadfast mercy (Gen. 18:25; Ps. 89:14). He calls sinners to repentance and promises forgiveness to all who come to Christ in faith. This truth steadies the church, sobers the conscience, and proclaims hope grounded in the righteousness and grace of God.

Conclusion
Living in Light of the Coming Kingdom

The Story That Holds Every Doctrine Together

Christian doctrine is not a collection of isolated truths scattered across Scripture. It is a single, coherent story centered on the triune God, who creates, redeems, and consummates all things in Jesus Christ.[208] The chapters of this book have traced key doctrines of the last things—from the fate of the unevangelized to the final judgment of the wicked and the eternal blessedness of the righteous—not as speculative charts but as chapters within God's great narrative.

At the heart of that story stands the crucified and risen Christ. The New Testament presents Him as the Alpha and Omega, the beginning and the end, the One in whom all God's purposes find their "Yes" (Rev. 22:13; 2 Cor. 1:20). From the promise in Genesis that the seed of the woman will crush the serpent's head (Gen. 3:15) to the vision of the Lamb enthroned in Revelation (Rev. 5:6-13), Scripture moves toward one climactic reality: the full and final reign of God in Christ, with His people, in a renewed creation.[209]

Every doctrine considered in the latter chapters of this book takes its meaning from this Christ-centered story. The fate of the unevangelized confronts us with the uniqueness of Christ and the urgency of the gospel. The Second Coming proclaims that history will not simply drift, but will be brought to its appointed goal by the return of the risen Lord. The rapture debates, the tribulation, and the climactic struggle of history highlight that Christian hope is realistic about suffering and sober about opposition, yet unwavering in confidence that Christ will triumph. The judgment reveals God's unwavering commitment to justice, while the eternal blessedness of the righteous displays the fullness of His mercy. The judgment of the wicked, hard as it is to contemplate, reminds us that sin is not a minor blemish but a revolt against the holy God.

Throughout, Scripture insists that eschatology is not merely about what will happen "someday," but about how believers live now. As one evangelical theologian has emphasized, the doctrine of last things "dominates and permeates the entire message of the Bible," because the future God has promised already presses in upon the present.[210] The kingdom has been inaugurated in Christ's first coming, even as we await its consummation at His return. We live in the tension of the "already" and the "not yet," called to faithful witness in the meantime.

Christ's Return: The Anchor of Christian Hope

The confession that "Christ will come again" stands near the center of Christian faith. The New Testament does not treat the return of Christ as a speculative add-on, but as a blessed hope that shapes the church's worship, ethics, and mission (Titus 2:11-13).[211] Whatever differences exist among believers regarding the timing of the rapture, the nature of the millennium, or the details of the tribulation, historic evangelical faith has agreed on several core convictions:

- Jesus Christ will return personally, visibly, and gloriously.

- His return will bring resurrection, judgment, and the renewal of creation.

- His coming will vindicate the righteous, defeat evil, and reveal the fullness of His reign.[212]

Because of this, Christian hope is not vague optimism, but confident expectation. Believers are not called to calculate dates but to cultivate readiness. Jesus' repeated admonitions—"Stay awake" (Matt. 24:42), "You also must be ready" (Matt. 24:44)—summon the church to a posture of watchful obedience. The certainty of His return gives weight to every choice, infuses suffering with purpose, and anchors joy beyond the contingencies of the present age.

The hope of Christ's coming also guards believers from two opposite errors: despair and presumption.[213] Despair forgets that the risen Christ reigns and will set all things right; presumption forgets that He will come as Judge as well as Savior. The New Testament holds these truths together. Believers are taught to "wait for his Son from heaven" who "delivers us from the wrath to come" (1 Thess. 1:10), even as they live in reverent fear, knowing they will give an account (2 Cor. 5:10).

Mission in a World That Needs the Gospel

Several chapters in this book have highlighted the tension between God's universal revelation and the particularity of the gospel. The question of the unevangelized, the reality of final judgment, and the doctrine of hell converge to press the church toward mission rather than speculation.

Scripture affirms that God has made Himself known in creation and conscience, so that all people are "without excuse" (Rom. 1:19-20). Yet it also proclaims that the gospel is "the power of God for salvation to everyone who believes" (Rom. 1:16) and that "faith comes from hearing, and hearing through the word of Christ" (Rom. 10:17). The ordinary pattern revealed in the New Testament is clear: God saves sinners through the proclamation of Christ crucified and risen.

This reality does not authorize the church to speak where Scripture is silent about the eternal destiny of specific individuals who may never have heard the gospel. It does, however, decisively shape where the church places its hope. Rather than resting in hypothetical exceptions, believers are called to rest in God's revealed way of salvation and to give themselves to making that way known "to the end of the earth" (Acts 1:8).[214]

A sober doctrine of judgment intensifies, rather than dulls, the urgency of mission. Knowing the "terror of the Lord," Paul writes, "we persuade others" (2 Cor. 5:11). The reality of hell is not an embarrassment to be hidden, but a reason to speak of Christ with tears, compassion, and urgency. As one evangelical writer has observed, the biblical teaching on eternal punishment "deepens our sense of the horror of sin and the greatness of grace," driving us both to worship and witness.[215]

At the same time, belief in God's sovereign justice frees Christians from the illusion that they must secure perfect outcomes. The Judge of all the earth will do right (Gen. 18:25). He knows every heart, weighs every opportunity, and will never wrong a single soul. This confidence allows believers to engage in evangelism with urgency and humility, trusting both the seriousness of judgment and the wideness of God's mercy in Christ.[216]

Hope, Holiness, and Perseverance

Biblical eschatology is relentlessly ethical. The New Testament never treats teaching about the future as mere information; it always presses that teaching into the shape of a transformed life. "What sort of people ought you to be," Peter asks, "in lives of holiness and godliness, waiting and hastening the coming of the day of God" (2 Pet. 3:11-12).[217]

The doctrines explored in these chapters call believers to a distinct way of life:

Hope in suffering. The prospect of tribulation, persecution, and the climactic struggle of history is not intended to paralyze the church, but to prepare it. Jesus warned His disciples that "in the world you will have tribulation. But take heart; I have overcome the world" (John 16:33). The promise of resurrection and the certainty of Christ's victory sustain believers in the face of loss, injustice, and opposition.

Serious about holiness. The Final Judgment, the judgment seat of Christ, and the doctrine of rewards remind believers that grace does not make obedience optional; it makes it possible. Salvation is by grace alone, through faith alone, in Christ alone, yet "we must all appear before the judgment seat of Christ" (2 Cor. 5:10). Good works do not earn salvation, but they demonstrate its reality and will be honored by the Lord.[218]

Gentle and compassionate. A right view of judgment and hell should never produce hardness or delight in the fate of the wicked. Scripture insists that God "does not willingly afflict or grieve the children of men" (Lam. 3:33) and takes "no pleasure in the death of the wicked" (Ezek. 33:11). Believers who share that heart will speak of judgment with gravity and tears, not with superiority.

Resilient in ordinary faithfulness. The promise of a new creation and eternal blessedness infuses daily work and ordinary obedience with significance. Because "in the Lord your labor is not in vain" (1 Cor. 15:58), Christians can persevere in unseen acts of service, quiet endurance in suffering, and costly faithfulness in hostile contexts. The future reign of Christ gives meaning to present faithfulness.

The Glory of Christ in Judgment and Salvation

One of the recurring themes in these chapters is that Christ Himself stands at the center of every eschatological event. He is the One through whom God will judge the world in righteousness (Acts 17:31). He is the One into whose presence believers are gathered, whose likeness they will bear, and whose glory will fill the renewed creation (Phil. 3:20-21; Rev. 21:22-23).

This Christ-centeredness guards the church from two distortions. First, it prevents us from treating eschatology as a system of impersonal processes. The future is not driven by abstract forces but by the personal reign of the crucified and risen Lord. Second, it prevents us from conceiving of salvation as a minimal escape from judgment rather than the fullness of life with Christ. Eternal blessedness is not merely the absence of pain; it is the presence of the triune God, the vision of His glory, and participation in His reign.[219]

The same is true on the side of judgment. Hell is not primarily the loss of created goods, but exclusion from the gracious presence of God and the encounter with His holy wrath (2 Thess. 1:8-9). The gravity of this reality can only be understood in light of the worth of the One who is rejected. Sin is horrific because God is infinitely worthy; judgment is severe because His holiness is not negotiable.

Yet precisely here the cross shines brightest. The One who will judge the living and the dead is the same One who "bore our sins in his body on the tree" (1 Pet. 2:24). At the cross, final judgment intruded into history, and the wrath of God was poured out on the innocent Son in place of guilty sinners.[220] Every doctrine of last things must be read through that lens. The final separation between the righteous and the wicked will reveal, not a failure of grace, but the outworking of grace rejected or received.

Worship, Awe, and the Fear of the Lord

A biblical doctrine of the future is meant to produce worship. The scenes of heaven in Revelation are filled with songs that celebrate both God's creation and His acts of judgment and salvation (Rev. 4-5; 19:1-2). The elders and living creatures fall down before the throne, crying, "worthy are you, our Lord and God, to receive glory and honor and power" (Rev. 4:11).

Contemplating the eternal blessedness of the righteous should lead believers to joyful anticipation: "We will see his face" (Rev. 22:4). This hope invites doxological wonder. As one evangelical writer has put it, the promise of seeing God and dwelling with Him forever "is the central joy of heaven, the fountain from which all other blessings flow."[221]

At the same time, the doctrine of hell and the judgment of the wicked summons believers to the fear of the Lord. This fear is not the dread of a capricious deity, but the reverent awe of a holy God who is not to be trifled with. Jesus Himself urged His disciples, "Do not fear those who kill the body but cannot kill the soul. Rather fear him who can destroy both soul and body in hell" (Matt. 10:28). Such fear is the beginning of wisdom, driving believers to cling more tightly to Christ and to flee from sin.[222]

Worship and awe belong together. The more deeply believers grasp the holiness and justice of God, the more they marvel at His mercy. The more seriously they take the warnings of judgment, the more they treasure the promises of grace. Eschatology, rightly taught, enlarges both our sense of God's greatness and our gratitude for His kindness.

Living Between the Times

Until Christ returns, the church lives "between the times" — between the accomplishment of redemption at the cross and the consummation of that redemption at His coming. This in-between time is marked by tension: victory has been won, yet battles remain; the kingdom has come, yet its fullness is still future; believers are new creatures, yet they struggle with sin.

The doctrines explored in this book equip Christians to live faithfully in this tension. Knowing that history is moving toward the renewal of creation frees believers from both utopian illusions and cynical despair. They are neither surprised by suffering nor resigned to it. They can work for justice, care for creation, and love their neighbors, knowing that their efforts anticipate the world that is coming, even as they await the day when Christ will do perfectly what they can only begin.[223]

Living between the times also shapes the way believers view their own mortality. Death remains an enemy (1 Cor. 15:26), but it is a defeated enemy. Those who die in Christ are "away from the body and at home with the Lord" (2 Cor. 5:8), awaiting the resurrection of the body and the renewal of all things. Grief is real, but it is not hopeless (1 Thess. 4:13-18).[224] The doctrines of the intermediate state, resurrection, and eternal life together provide a framework in which Christian funerals can be both honest about loss and filled with hope.

The Last Word Belongs to God

In the end, the doctrine of last things reminds the church that the last word about history, humanity, sin, and salvation does not belong to governments, cultures, or individuals; it belongs to God. He is the One who began the story in creation, the One who entered the story in the incarnation, and the One who will bring the story to its appointed conclusion at the return of Christ.

For the righteous, that last word will be "Well done…enter into the joy of your master" (Matt. 25:21). For the wicked, it will be a word of just judgment. For the whole creation, it will mean liberation from bondage to decay and entrance into "the freedom of the glory of the children of God" (Rom. 8:21).

Until that day, the church prays the final prayer of Scripture: "Amen. Come, Lord Jesus!" (Rev. 22:20).[225] That prayer, whispered in suffering, sung in worship, and carried in hope, sums up the entire message of this book. Christ has come. Christ will come again. Between His comings, believers are called to faith, obedience, witness, and worship, confident that "he who calls you is faithful; he will surely do it" (1 Thess. 5:24).

Endnotes

Chapter 1

[1] N. T. Wright, *Surprised by Hope: Rethinking Heaven, the Resurrection, and the Mission of the Church* (New York: HarperOne, 2008), 92-115.

[2] Richard Bauckham, *The Theology of the Book of Revelation* (Cambridge: Cambridge University Press, 1993), 31-54.

[3] Oscar Cullmann, *Christ and Time: The Primitive Christian Concept of Time and History*, rev. ed. (London: SCM Press, 1967), 84-99.

[4] Anthony A. Hoekema, *The Bible and the Future* (Grand Rapids: Eerdmans, 1979), 3-14.

[5] Cullmann, *Christ and Time*, 51-70.

[6] Hoekema, *The Bible and the Future*, 59-79.

[7] Cullmann, *Christ and Time*, 103-18.

[8] Geerhardus Vos, *Biblical Theology: Old and New Testaments* (Edinburgh: Banner of Truth, 1975), 325-39.

[9] Wright, *Surprised by Hope*, 55-78.

[10] Cullmann, *Christ and Time*, 119-35.

[11] Hoekema, *The Bible and the Future*, 83-112.

[12] Wright, *Surprised by Hope*, 103-32.

[13] *Ibid.*, 147-70.

[14] Vos, *Biblical Theology*, 115-30.

[15] Walter C. Kaiser Jr., *The Messiah in the Old Testament* (Grand Rapids: Zondervan, 1995), 89-103.

[16] Tremper Longman III, *Daniel*, NIV Application Commentary (Grand Rapids: Zondervan, 1999), 77-88, 177-90.

[17] John N. Oswalt, *The Book of Isaiah, Chapters 1-39*, NICOT (Grand Rapids: Eerdmans, 1986), 117-24, 275-86.

[18] George Eldon Ladd, *The Gospel of the Kingdom: Scriptural Studies in the Kingdom of God* (Grand Rapids: Eerdmans, 1959), 17-23.

[19] George Eldon Ladd, *A Theology of the New Testament*, rev. ed., ed. Donald A. Hagner (Grand Rapids: Eerdmans, 1993), 91-101.

[20] *Ibid.*, 613-26.

[21] Wright, *Surprised by Hope*, 207-22.

Chapter 2

[22] Ladd, *The Gospel of the Kingdom*, 18-21.

[23] *Ibid.*, 20-23.

[24] Ladd, *A Theology of the New Testament*, 91-93.

[25] David H. J. Gay, "Our Priest in the Pattern of Melchizedek: Eight Conclusions Hebrews 5-7 Draws about Jesus," *Christ Over All*, May 6, 2024, https://christoverall.com/article, concise/our-priest-in-the-pattern-of-melchizedek-eight-conclusions-hebrews-5-7-draws-about-jesus/.

[26] G. K. Beale, *The Book of Revelation: A Commentary on the Greek Text*, New International Greek Testament Commentary (Grand Rapids: Eerdmans, 1999), 347-50.

27 Vos, *Biblical Theology*, 139-52.

28 N. T. Wright, *Jesus and the Victory of God* (Minneapolis: Fortress Press, 1996), 201-24.

29 *Ibid.*, 227-39.

30 Ladd, *The Gospel of the Kingdom*, 55-71.

31 Geerhardus Vos, *The Teaching of Jesus Concerning the Kingdom of God and the Church* (Grand Rapids: Eerdmans, 1951), 77-90.

32 Ladd, *A Theology of the New Testament*, 109-13.

33 David Schrock, "George Eldon Ladd on 'The Kingdom and the Church,'" *Christ Over All* (blog), May 30, 2016, https://davidschrock.com/2016/05/31/george-eldon-ladd-on-the-kingdom-and-the-church/.

34 David VanDrunen, "The Relationship between Church and Kingdom according to Geerhardus Vos," *Reformed Forum*, April 29, 2017, https://reformedforum.org/relationship-church-kingdom-according-geerhardus-vos/.

35 Bauckham, *The Theology of the Book of Revelation*, 72-92.

36 N. T. Wright, *How God Became King: The Forgotten Story of the Gospels* (New York: HarperOne, 2012), 113-37.

37 Wright, *Surprised by Hope*, 202-14.

38 Beale, *The Book of Revelation*, 347-60, 930-40.

39 Vos, *Biblical Theology*, 139-65.

Chapter 3

[40] Hoekema, *The Bible and the Future*, 13-21.

[41] Ladd, *The Presence of the Future*, 149-58.

[42] *Ibid.*, 218-25.

[43] Hoekema, *The Bible and the Future*, 41-53.

[44] Michael J. Vlach, "Premillennialism and Inaugurated Eschatology," in *The Meaning of the Millennium: Four Views*, ed. Robert G. Clouse (Downers Grove, IL: InterVarsity, 1977), 223-28; Hoekema, *The Bible and the Future*, 174-79.

[45] Ladd, *The Presence of the Future*, 121-30.

[46] Hoekema, *The Bible and the Future*, 10-12.

[47] Ladd, *The Presence of the Future*, 131-38.

[48] Hoekema, *The Bible and the Future*, 12-13.

[49] Ladd, *The Presence of the Future*, 139-46.

[50] Hoekema, *The Bible and the Future*, 13-21; Ladd, *The Presence of the Future*, 218-25.

[51] Oscar Cullmann, *Christ and Time*, 84-99; Fred G. Zaspel, "D-Day and V-E Day," *Credo Magazine*, June 8, 2013, https://credomag.com/2013/09/d-day-and-ve-day-fred-zaspel/.

[52] Hoekema, *The Bible and the Future*, 13-21, 237-55; Ladd, *The Presence of the Future*, 328-39.

[53] Ladd, *The Presence of the Future*, 261-70.

[54] Hoekema, *The Bible and the Future*, 247-55.

55 Hoekema, *The Bible and the Future*, 13-21; Ladd, *The Presence of the Future*, 328-39.

Chapter 4

56 Wayne Grudem, *Systematic Theology: An Introduction to Biblical Doctrine*, 2nd ed. (Grand Rapids: Zondervan, 2020), 1117-19; Millard J. Erickson, *Christian Theology*, 3rd ed. (Grand Rapids: Baker Academic, 2013), 1195-96.

57 Beale, *The Book of Revelation*, 972-83.

58 Grudem, *Systematic Theology*, 1119-22.

59 Hoekema, *The Bible and the Future*, 176-79.

60 Erickson, *Christian Theology*, 1204-7.

61 Grudem, *Systematic Theology*, 1119-22; Hoekema, *The Bible and the Future*, 178-82.

62 Erickson, *Christian Theology*, 1200-02.

63 Hoekema, *The Bible and the Future*, 175-76.

64 Erickson, *Christian Theology*, 1196-98.

65 Beale, *The Book of Revelation*, 972-83; Hoekema, *The Bible and the Future*, 226-31.

66 Grudem, *Systematic Theology*, 1119-22.

67 Grudem, *Systematic Theology*, 1115-17; Erickson, *Christian Theology*, 1195-96.

Chapter 5

[68] Hoekema, *The Bible and the Future*, 274-85.

[69] *Ibid.*, 280-282.

[70] Grudem, *Systematic Theology*, 1158-60.

[71] Hoekema, *The Bible and the Future*, 45-55.

[72] Grudem, *Systematic Theology*, 1159-60; Hoekema, *The Bible and the Future*, 201-7.

[73] Wright, *Surprised by Hope*, 85-94.

[74] Beale, *The Book of Revelation*, 1041-52; Hoekema, *The Bible and the Future*, 286-96.

[75] Hoekema, *The Bible and the Future*, 45-55, 274-85.

Chapter 6

[76] Hoekema, *The Bible and the Future*, 83-112, 249-55.

[77] Grudem, *Systematic Theology*, 1143-52; Hoekema, *The Bible and the Future*, 83-90, 274-85.

[78] Erickson, *Christian Theology*, 1179-82.

[79] Grudem, *Systematic Theology*, 1158-60; Hoekema, *The Bible and the Future*, 250-55.

[80] Hoekema, *The Bible and the Future*, 251-255; R. C. Sproul, *Essential Truths of the Christian Faith* (Wheaton, IL: Tyndale, 1992), 237-40.

[81] David S. Dockery, *Christianity's Textbook on Eschatology*, in *The Hope of Glory: Essays in Honor of David S. Dockery*, ed. Timothy George and Nathan Finn (Nashville: B&H Academic, 2014), 45-52.

[82] Randy Alcorn, *Heaven* (Carol Stream, IL: Tyndale, 2004), 138-57.

[83] John Calvin, *Institutes of the Christian Religion*, 3.25.6-16; Erickson, *Christian Theology*, 1185-90.

[84] Grudem, *Systematic Theology*, 1143-52; Stephen J. Wellum, "Death and the Intermediate State," in *Biblical Doctrine*, ed. John MacArthur and Richard Mayhue (Wheaton, IL: Crossway, 2017).

[85] Hoekema, *The Bible and the Future*, 83-90; Grudem, *Systematic Theology*, 1143-45.

[86] Wright, *Surprised by Hope*, 197-222; Sproul, *Essential Truths of the Christian Faith*, 237-40.

[87] Hoekema, *The Bible and the Future*, 274-85; Alcorn, *Heaven*, 17-30.

Chapter 7

[88] Hoekema, *The Bible and the Future*, 274-85; Grudem, *Systematic Theology*, 1158-63.

[89] Hoekema, *The Bible and the Future*, 67-73.

[90] Grudem, *Systematic Theology*, 372-75; Erickson, *Christian Theology*, 412-15.

[91] Sproul, *Essential Truths of the Christian Faith*, 219-23.

[92] Wright, *Surprised by Hope*, 148-61.

[93] Alcorn, *Heaven*, 124-45; Hoekema, *The Bible and the Future*, 274-80.

[94] Hoekema, *The Bible and the Future*, 274-85; Grudem, *Systematic Theology*, 1158-63.

⁹⁵ David S. Dockery, ed., *Theologians of the Baptist Tradition* (Nashville: B&H Academic, 2011), 317-23; Erickson, *Christian Theology*, 1180-86.

⁹⁶ Wright, *Surprised by Hope*, 197-222; Alcorn, *Heaven*, 17-30.

Chapter 8

⁹⁷ Hoekema, *The Bible and the Future*, 258-63.

⁹⁸ Grudem, *Systematic Theology*, 1165-70.

⁹⁹ Hoekema, *The Bible and the Future*, 266-72; Erickson, *Christian Theology*, 1234-39.

¹⁰⁰ Hoekema, *The Bible and the Future*, 23-32.

¹⁰¹ D. A. Carson, "Matthew," in *The Expositor's Bible Commentary*, rev. ed., vol. 9, ed. Tremper Longman III and David E. Garland (Grand Rapids: Zondervan, 2010), 156-58.

¹⁰² Sproul, *Essential Truths of the Christian Faith*, 222-25.

¹⁰³ Hoekema, *The Bible and the Future*, 266-72; Grudem, *Systematic Theology*, 1165-70.

¹⁰⁴ Christopher W. Morgan and Robert A. Peterson, eds., *Hell Under Fire: Modern Scholarship Reinvents Eternal Punishment* (Grand Rapids: Zondervan, 2004), 197-220.

¹⁰⁵ Grudem, *Systematic Theology*, 1165-70; Erickson, *Christian Theology*, 1234-39.

¹⁰⁶ John Stott and David L. Edwards, *Evangelical Essentials: A Liberal-Evangelical Dialogue* (Downers Grove, IL: InterVarsity, 1988), 314-18 (Stott's discussion on judgment and the cross).

107 David S. Dockery, "Evangelism and the Doctrine of Hell," in *The Great Commission: Evangelicals and the History of World Missions*, ed. Martin I. Klauber and Scott M. Manetsch (Nashville: B&H Academic, 2008), 189-203.

108 Hoekema, *The Bible and the Future*, 263-66.

Chapter 9

109 Morgan and Peterson, eds., *Faith Comes by Hearing*, 17-22.

110 Grudem, *Systematic Theology*, 493-98.

111 Erickson, *Christian Theology*, 211-15.

112 Hoekema, *The Bible and the Future*, 399-404; Grudem, *Systematic Theology*, 552-59.

113 Morgan and Peterson, *Faith Comes by Hearing*, 49-66.

114 R. Albert Mohler Jr., "A Theology of the Exclusivity of Christ," in *Faith Comes by Hearing*, 125-43.

115 D. A. Carson, *The Gagging of God: Christianity Confronts Pluralism* (Grand Rapids: Zondervan, 1996), 300-332.

116 John Piper, *Let the Nations Be Glad! The Supremacy of God in Missions*, 4th ed. (Grand Rapids: Baker Academic, 2010), 124-36.

117 Grudem, *Systematic Theology*, 493-98, 552-59, 986-93.

118 Morgan and Peterson, *Faith Comes by Hearing*, 23-32.

119 Piper, *Let the Nations Be Glad!*, 120-24.

120 David S. Dockery, "Missions and the Exclusivity of Christ," in *Faith Comes by Hearing*, 203-19.

[121] Erickson, *Christian Theology*, 215-18.

Chapter 10

[122] Hoekema, *The Bible and the Future*, 13-18, 168-73.

[123] Grudem, *Systematic Theology*, 1131-35.

[124] Hoekema, *The Bible and the Future*, 168-73; Erickson, *Christian Theology*, 120-25.

[125] George Eldon Ladd, *The Presence of the Future: The Eschatology of Biblical Realism* (Grand Rapids: Eerdmans, 1974), 217-26.

[126] Grudem, *Systematic Theology*, 1131-33.

[127] Hoekema, *The Bible and the Future*, 174-80.

[128] Erickson, *Christian Theology*, 1159-63.

[129] John Piper, *Future Grace* (Sisters, OR: Multnomah, 1995), 381-89.

[130] Sproul, *Essential Truths of the Christian Faith*, 229-33.

[131] Hoekema, *The Bible and the Future*, 13-18; Grudem, *Systematic Theology*, 1131-35.

Chapter 11

[132] Hoekema, *The Bible and the Future*, 168-73.

[133] Grudem, *Systematic Theology*, 1136-39.

[134] Erickson, *Christian Theology*, 1239-44.

[135] Hoekema, *The Bible and the Future*, 168-72.

[136] Grudem, *Systematic Theology*, 1136-39.

[137] John F. Walvoord, *The Rapture Question*, rev. and enlarged ed. (Grand Rapids: Zondervan, 1979), 23-34.

[138] Craig A. Blaising and Darrell L. Bock, eds., *Three Views on the Rapture: Pre-, Mid-, or Post-Tribulation?* (Grand Rapids: Zondervan, 1996), 7-15.

[139] Hoekema, *The Bible and the Future*, 174-80.

[140] Kenneth L. Gentry Jr., *He Shall Have Dominion: A Postmillennial Eschatology*, 3rd ed. (Draper, VA: Apologetics Group Media, 2009), 287-95.

[141] Grudem, *Systematic Theology*, 1131-39; Erickson, *Christian Theology*, 1239-44.

[142] Hoekema, *The Bible and the Future*, 171-73.

[143] Douglas J. Moo, "Eschatology and the Christian's Life," in *The Return of Christ: A Premillennial Perspective*, ed. David R. Anderson (Nashville: B&H Academic, 2011), 269-80.

[144] Hoekema, *The Bible and the Future*, 168-80; Grudem, *Systematic Theology*, 1131-39.

Chapter 12

[145] Hoekema, *The Bible and the Future*, 244-50.

[146] Grudem, *Systematic Theology*, 1139-44.

[147] Hoekema, *The Bible and the Future*, 244-50; Grudem, *Systematic Theology*, 1139-44.

[148] John F. Walvoord, *Daniel: The Key to Prophetic Revelation* (Chicago: Moody, 1971), 219-37; Hoekema, *The Bible and the Future*, 167-73.

[149] Beale, *The Book of Revelation*, 104-12.

[150] Walvoord, *The Rapture Question*, 123-39.

[151] Ladd, *The Blessed Hope*, 153-68.

[152] R. C. Sproul, *The Last Days According to Jesus* (Grand Rapids: Baker, 1998), 61-89.

[153] Hoekema, *The Bible and the Future*, 244-50.

[154] Grudem, *Systematic Theology*, 1144-49.

[155] Beale, *The Book of Revelation*, 628-35.

[156] David S. Dockery, "Eschatology and Christian Perseverance," in *The Hope of Glory: Essays in Honor of David S. Dockery*, ed. Timothy George and Nathan Finn (Nashville: B&H Academic, 2014), 221-32.

[157] Grudem, *Systematic Theology*, 1139-49; Erickson, *Christian Theology*, 1190-98.

Chapter 13

[158] Hoekema, *The Bible and the Future*, 13-18, 255-60.

[159] Grudem, *Systematic Theology*, 1152-57.

[160] Erickson, *Christian Theology*, 1230-37.

[161] Hoekema, *The Bible and the Future*, 255-60.

[162] Grudem, *Systematic Theology*, 1153-55.

[163] Hoekema, *The Bible and the Future*, 261-66.

[164] Beale, *The Book of Revelation*, 1012-17.

[165] Sproul, *Essential Truths of the Christian Faith*, 224-28.

[166] John Murray, *Redemption Accomplished and Applied* (Grand Rapids: Eerdmans, 1955), 119-28; Grudem, *Systematic Theology*, 748-52.

[167] Erickson, *Christian Theology*, 1237-40.

[168] Hoekema, *The Bible and the Future*, 262-66.

[169] Carson, *The Gagging of God*, 517-22.

[170] Hoekema, *The Bible and the Future*, 263-66.

[171] Beale, *The Book of Revelation*, 955-63, 1012-17.

[172] Hoekema, *The Bible and the Future*, 274-81; Grudem, *Systematic Theology*, 1157-63.

[173] John Piper, *Future Grace*, 381-89.

[174] Erickson, *Christian Theology*, 1240-44.

Chapter 14

[175] Hoekema, *The Bible and the Future*, 266-73.

[176] Grudem, *Systematic Theology*, 1158-63.

[177] Erickson, *Christian Theology*, 1245-52.

[178] Hoekema, *The Bible and the Future*, 99-115, 249-55.

[179] N. T. Wright, *The Resurrection of the Son of God* (Minneapolis: Fortress, 2003), 710-13.

[180] Erickson, *Christian Theology*, 1237-40.

[181] Hoekema, *The Bible and the Future*, 261-66.

[182] Grudem, *Systematic Theology*, 1158-60.

[183] Hoekema, *The Bible and the Future*, 274-81; John Calvin, *Institutes of the Christian Religion*, 3.25.1-5.

[184] Stephen J. Wellum, "The Glory of God in Salvation," in *The Glory of God*, ed. Christopher W. Morgan and Robert A. Peterson (Wheaton, IL: Crossway, 2010), 251-56.

[185] Randy Alcorn, *Heaven*, 157-70.

[186] Grudem, *Systematic Theology*, 1158-60; Wright, *The Resurrection of the Son of God*, 607-19.

[187] Erickson, *Christian Theology*, 1248-52.

[188] Hoekema, *The Bible and the Future*, 274-81.

[189] Grudem, *Systematic Theology*, 1157-63.

[190] Alcorn, *Heaven*, 173-92.

[191] Hoekema, *The Bible and the Future*, 266-73.

[192] John Piper, *Future Grace*, 381-89.

Chapter 15

[193] Hoekema, *The Bible and the Future*, 253-60.

[194] Grudem, *Systematic Theology*, 1149-52.

[195] Erickson, *Christian Theology*, 1218-23.

[196] John Murray, *The Epistle to the Romans*, NICNT (Grand Rapids: Eerdmans, 1968), 1:37-42.

[197] Carson, *The Gagging of God*, 516-22.

[198] Hoekema, *The Bible and the Future*, 255-60.

[199] Grudem, *Systematic Theology*, 1150-52.

[200] Hoekema, *The Bible and the Future*, 260-66.

[201] Robert A. Peterson, *Hell on Trial: The Case for Eternal Punishment* (Phillipsburg, NJ: P&R, 1995), 175-92.

[202] Erickson, *Christian Theology*, 1230-37.

[203] Hoekema, *The Bible and the Future*, 266-73.

[204] Gene L. Green, *The Letters to the Thessalonians*, PNTC (Grand Rapids: Eerdmans, 2002), 294-99.

[205] Christopher W. Morgan and Robert A. Peterson, eds., *Hell Under Fire: Modern Scholarship Reinvents Eternal Punishment* (Grand Rapids: Zondervan, 2004), 15-32.

[206] R. Albert Mohler Jr., "Modern Theology: The Disappearance of Hell," in *Hell Under Fire*, 15-34.

[207] Piper, *Let the Nations Be Glad!*, 120-29.

Conclusion
[208] Hoekema, *The Bible and the Future*, 9-18.

[209] Grudem, *Systematic Theology*, 1131-35, 1157-63.

[210] Ladd, *The Presence of the Future*, 321-29.

[211] Grudem, *Systematic Theology*, 1131-39.

[212] Hoekema, *The Bible and the Future*, 168-80.

[213] Erickson, *Christian Theology*, 120-25, 1230-37.

[214] Morgan and Peterson, eds., *Faith Comes by Hearing*, 17-32.

[215] Piper, *Let the Nations Be Glad!*, 120-29.

[216] Erickson, *Christian Theology*, 1230-37.

[217] Grudem, *Systematic Theology*, 1150-52.

[218] Hoekema, *The Bible and the Future*, 261-66.

[219] Hoekema, *The Bible and the Future*, 266-73; Grudem, *Systematic Theology*, 1157-63.

[220] Murray, *Redemption Accomplished and Applied*, 25-35.

[221] Alcorn, *Heaven*, 157-70.

[222] Peterson, *Hell on Trial*, 175-92.

[223] Hoekema, *The Bible and the Future*, 274-81.

[224] Erickson, *Christian Theology*, 1245-52.

[225] Grudem, *Systematic Theology*, 1131-39.

Selected Bibliography and Works Consulted

Akin, Daniel L., ed. *A Theology for the Church*. Revised ed. Associate editors Bruce Riley Ashford and Kenneth Keathley. Nashville: B&H Publishing Group, 2014.

Alcorn, Randy. *Heaven*. Carol Stream, IL: Tyndale, 2004.

Anderson, David R., ed. *The Return of Christ: A Premillennial Perspective*. Nashville: B&H Academic, 2011.

Bauckham, Richard. *The Theology of the Book of Revelation*. Cambridge: Cambridge University Press, 1993.

Beale, G. K. *The Book of Revelation: A Commentary on the Greek Text*. New International Greek Testament Commentary. Grand Rapids: Eerdmans, 1999.

Blaising, Craig A., and Darrell L. Bock, eds. *Three Views on the Rapture: Pre-, Mid-, or Post-Tribulation?* Grand Rapids: Zondervan, 1996.

Bloesch, Donald G. *Essentials of Evangelical Theology, Volume One: God, Authority, and Salvation*. New York: Harper & Row, 1978.

Calvin, John. *Institutes of the Christian Religion*. Translated by Henry Beveridge. Peabody, MA: Hendrickson Publishers, 2012.

Carson, D. A. *The Gagging of God: Christianity Confronts Pluralism*. Grand Rapids: Zondervan, 1996.

_____. "Matthew." In *The Expositor's Bible Commentary*. Rev. ed. vol. 9. Edited by Tremper Longman III and David E. Garland. Grand Rapids: Zondervan, 2010.

Clouse, Robert G., ed. *The Meaning of the Millennium: Four Views*. Downers Grove, IL: InterVarsity Press, 1977.

Conner, W. T. *Christian Doctrine*. Nashville: Broadman Press, 1937.

Cullmann, Oscar. *Christ and Time: The Primitive Christian Concept of Time and History*. Rev. ed. London: SCM Press, 1967.

Dockery, David S. "Christianity's Textbook on Eschatology." In *The Hope of Glory: Essays in Honor of David S. Dockery*, edited by Timothy George and Nathan Finn. Nashville: B&H Academic, 2014.

_____. "Eschatology and Christian Perseverance." In *The Hope of Glory: Essays in Honor of David S. Dockery*, edited by Timothy George and Nathan Finn. Nashville: B&H Academic, 2014.

_____. "Evangelism and the Doctrine of Hell." In *The Great Commission: Evangelicals and the History of World Missions*, edited by Martin I. Klauber and Scott M. Manetsch. Nashville: B&H Academic, 2008.

_____. ed. *Theologians of the Baptist Tradition*. Nashville: B&H Academic, 2011.

Eddleman, H. Leo, ed. *Last Things: A Symposium of Prophetic Messages*. Grand Rapids: Zondervan, 1969.

Edwards, David L., and John Stott. *Evangelical Essentials: A Liberal-Evangelical Dialogue*. Downers Grove, IL: InterVarsity Press, 1988.

Erickson, Millard J. *Christian Theology*. 3rd ed. Grand Rapids: Baker Academic, 2013.

Gay, David H. J. "Our Priest in the Pattern of Melchizedek: Eight Conclusions Hebrews 5–7 Draws about Jesus." *Christ Over All*. May 6, 2024.

Gentry, Kenneth L., Jr. *He Shall Have Dominion: A Postmillennial Eschatology*. 3rd ed. Draper, VA: Apologetics Group Media, 2009.

George, Timothy, and Nathan Finn, eds. *The Hope of Glory: Essays in Honor of David S. Dockery*. Nashville: B&H Academic, 2014.

Green, Gene L. *The Letters to the Thessalonians*. Pillar New Testament Commentary. Grand Rapids: Eerdmans, 2002.

Grudem, Wayne. *Biblical Doctrine: Essential Teachings of the Christian Faith*. Edited by Jeff Purswell. Grand Rapids: Zondervan, 1999.

———. *Systematic Theology: An Introduction to Biblical Doctrine*. 2nd ed. Grand Rapids: Zondervan, 2020.

Hoekema, Anthony A. *The Bible and the Future*. Grand Rapids: Eerdmans, 1979.

Kaiser, Walter C., Jr. *The Messiah in the Old Testament*. Grand Rapids: Zondervan, 1995.

King, Max R. *The Cross and the Parousia of Christ: The Two Dimensions of One Age-Changing Eschaton*. [n.p.]: Writing and Research Ministry, 1987.

Klauber, Martin I., and Scott M. Manetsch, eds. *The Great Commission: Evangelicals and the History of World Missions*. Nashville: B&H Academic, 2008.

Ladd, George Eldon. *The Blessed Hope: A Biblical Study of the Second Advent and the Rapture*. Grand Rapids: Eerdmans, 1956.

———. *The Gospel of the Kingdom: Scriptural Studies in the Kingdom of God*. Grand Rapids: Eerdmans, 1959.

———. *The Presence of the Future: The Eschatology of Biblical Realism*. Grand Rapids: Eerdmans, 1974.

———. *A Theology of the New Testament*. Rev. ed. Edited by Donald A. Hagner. Grand Rapids: Eerdmans, 1993.

Lexham Survey of Theology. General editors Brannon Ellis and Mark Ward; technical editor Jessica Parks. *Lexham Survey of Theology*. Bellingham, WA: Lexham Press, 2018. Logos digital edition.

Longman, Tremper III. *Daniel*. NIV Application Commentary. Grand Rapids: Zondervan, 1999.

MacArthur, John, and Richard Mayhue, eds. *Biblical Doctrine: A Systematic Summary of Bible Truth*. Wheaton, IL: Crossway, 2017.

Middleton, J. Richard. *A New Heaven and a New Earth: Reclaiming Biblical Eschatology*. Grand Rapids: Baker Academic, 2014.

Mohler, R. Albert, Jr. "A Theology of the Exclusivity of Christ." In *Faith Comes by Hearing: A Response to Inclusivism*, edited by Christopher W. Morgan and Robert A. Peterson. Downers Grove, IL: InterVarsity Press, 2008.

———. "Modern Theology: The Disappearance of Hell." In *Hell Under Fire: Modern Scholarship Reinvents Eternal Punishment*, edited by Christopher W. Morgan and Robert A. Peterson. Grand Rapids: Zondervan, 2004.

Moo, Douglas J. "Eschatology and the Christian's Life." In *The Return of Christ: A Premillennial Perspective*, edited by David R. Anderson. Nashville: B&H Academic, 2011.

Morgan, Christopher W., and Robert A. Peterson, eds. *Faith Comes by Hearing: A Response to Inclusivism*. Downers Grove, IL: InterVarsity Press, 2008.

———, eds. *Hell Under Fire: Modern Scholarship Reinvents Eternal Punishment*. Grand Rapids: Zondervan, 2004.

———, eds. *The Glory of God*. Wheaton, IL: Crossway, 2010.

Murray, John. *Redemption Accomplished and Applied*. Grand Rapids: Eerdmans, 1955.

———. *The Epistle to the Romans*. New International Commentary on the New Testament. Vol. 1. Grand Rapids: Eerdmans, 1968.

Oswalt, John N. *The Book of Isaiah, Chapters 1–39*. New International Commentary on the Old Testament. Grand Rapids: Eerdmans, 1986.

Peterson, Robert A. *Hell on Trial: The Case for Eternal Punishment*. Phillipsburg, NJ: P&R, 1995.

Pink, Arthur W. *The Doctrines of Election and Justification*. Grand Rapids: Baker Book House, 1974.

Piper, John. *Future Grace*. Sisters, OR: Multnomah, 1995.

———. *Let the Nations Be Glad! The Supremacy of God in Missions*. 4th ed. Grand Rapids: Baker Academic, 2010.

Schrock, David. "George Eldon Ladd on 'The Kingdom and the Church.'" *Christ Over All* (blog). May 30, 2016.

Smith, Ralph L. *Old Testament Theology: Its History, Method, and Message.* Nashville: Broadman & Holman Publishers, 1993.

Sproul, R. C. *Essential Truths of the Christian Faith.* Wheaton, IL: Tyndale, 1992.

_____. *The Last Days According to Jesus.* Grand Rapids: Baker, 1998.

Stagg, Frank. *New Testament Theology.* Nashville: Broadman Press, 1962.

VanDrunen, David. "The Relationship between Church and Kingdom according to Geerhardus Vos." *Reformed Forum.* April 29, 2017.

Vlach, Michael J. "Premillennialism and Inaugurated Eschatology." In *The Meaning of the Millennium: Four Views*, edited by Robert G. Clouse. Downers Grove, IL: InterVarsity Press, 1977.

Vos, Geerhardus. *Biblical Theology: Old and New Testaments.* Edinburgh: Banner of Truth, 1975.

_____. *The Teaching of Jesus Concerning the Kingdom of God and the Church.* Grand Rapids: Eerdmans, 1951.

Walvoord, John F. *Daniel: The Key to Prophetic Revelation.* Chicago: Moody, 1971.

_____. *The Rapture Question.* Rev. and enl. ed. Grand Rapids: Zondervan, 1979.

Wellum, Stephen J. *Systematic Theology: From Canon to Concept.* Vol. 1. Brentwood, TN: B&H Academic, 2024.

_____. "Death and the Intermediate State." In *Biblical Doctrine*, edited by John MacArthur and Richard Mayhue. Wheaton, IL: Crossway, 2017.

Wiley, H. Orton, and Paul T. Culbertson. *Introduction to Christian Theology.* Kansas City, MO: Beacon Hill Press of Kansas City, 1946.

Wright, N. T. *How God Became King: The Forgotten Story of the Gospels.* New York: HarperOne, 2012.

_____. *Jesus and the Victory of God.* Minneapolis: Fortress Press, 1996.

_____. *The Resurrection of the Son of God.* Minneapolis: Fortress Press, 2003.

_____. *Surprised by Hope: Rethinking Heaven, the Resurrection, and the Mission of the Church.* New York: HarperOne, 2008.

Zaspel, Fred G. "D-Day and V-E Day." *Credo Magazine.* June 8, 2013

www.ingramcontent.com/pod-product-compliance
Lightning Source LLC
LaVergne TN
LVHW041333080426
835512LV00006B/434